DEDICATION

To My Family and Friends,

You are the wind beneath my wings.

Thank you for your impact in my life.

CONTENTS

Introduction

The Story of Jael

There are moments in life that strike us in such a way that it stays with us forever. Such is the case when I read about Jael. Like me, Jael was just an ordinary woman going about her life. When I read the story of this woman named Jael in the Old Testament Book of Judges, it just never left me. Here is an average everyday person who carried out an act that saved an entire nation of people. This story struck me so deeply, because just like many of us, Jael was an everyday ordinary person. This is an Old Testament story found the the Holy Bible. It reveals how God can use us, in spite of the faults that we all have.

There are a lot of known characters in the Bible, but Jael is not one of them. Jael wasn't a judge like Judge Deborah or a queen like Queen Esther in the Old Testament, but a common everyday person. Jael's fame came from from one incident in which her courageous act won a victory for God's chosen people in Old Testament times. Jael's tribe, the Kenites, were living in peace and not at war with anyone. The Israelites, who are also called the children of Israel, and the Canaanites, were in battle.

1

In fact, prior to her story recorded in chapter four and chapter five in the Book of Judges, in a previous Old Testament book, Exodus, we read about the great miracles that the Lord performed in Egypt in freeing the children of Israel from slavery through Moses. Later, in chapter one of the Book of Joshua, after Moses' death, God commissioned Joshua as the children of Israel's new leader. Throughout all of this, God promised to give land to the children of Israel. However, in the Book of Judges, Israel's leadership was turned over to judges, and the children of Israel asked God in Judges 1:1, who would be the first to lead in the fight against the Canaanites. In verse two, God answered and said that He would deliver the Canaanites to Judah, who was the leader of one of the twelve tribes of Israel.

During this time in history when the children of Israel were under the leadership of judges, one such judge was a woman named Deborah. Judge Deborah called Barak to question him as to why he had not already gathered his men for battle based on God's promise. When Judge Deborah questioned her military leader, Barak, I am sure she expected a bold and confident response, but, Barak was scared. Barak told Deborah that he would only go if she went with him. Barak feared the commander of the Canaanites army, Sisera. Due to Barak's lack of courage, Deborah agreed to go with Barak, and she told him that the honor of the enemy's defeat would not be his, but instead the victory would come through the hands of a woman. I am sure Barak probably thought that Deborah was talking about herself. But little did Barak know that the words of Deborah were about to come to life in an unexpected way, and little did he know the power of God to work around his lack of courage. As we go on this journey, that is the first thing I want you to notice.

What Barak and his ten thousand soldiers could not do by slaying the enemy's commander, Sisera, Jael made it happen in just an instant. When Jael woke up that morning, I am sure she had no idea how God would use her in such a mighty way in the life of the Israelites. In the course of battle, Sisera jumped off of his chariot and fled on foot right to the tent of Jael. Knowing who he was, Jael invited him to hide in her tent, and she covered him with a blanket so he would feel safe. Jael provided him with warm milk that put him right to sleep. If you recall, God had promised to give the children of Israel the land. In spite of Barak's lack of courage, God raised up someone else to carry out His will. Jael, an ordinary woman, a tent dweller, took the peg from her tent and a hammer and pinned Sisera's head to the floor to win the war for the children of Israel. There are times when God will call us to be courageous to not only work through our own mistakes, but to work around other people's mistakes as well. In this case, because of Barak's lack of courage, God used this ordinary woman. Jael impacted history in such a way that it landed her name in the Bible with one courageous act that changed the course of a war. The people of her day revered her act so much that Judge Deborah and Barak celebrated her with a song.

> "Most blessed among women is Jael,
> The wife of Heber the Kenite:
> Blessed is she among women in tents.
> He asked for water, she gave him milk;
> She brought out cream in a lordly bowl.
> She stretched her hand to the tent peg.
> Her right hand to the workmen's hammer;
> She pounded Sisera, she pierced his head,
> She split and struck through his temple.
> At her feet he sank, he fell, he lay still;
> At her feet he sank, he fell;
> Where he sank, there he fell dead."   *~Judges 5:24-27*

Prior to Jael's action in winning the war, Deborah and Barak probably would not have even noticed she existed. Jael's story shows how our lives are so interwoven with each other. God can use the daily impact of our choices, even in our faults and even when we can't see the whole picture. Deborah, Barak and Jael existed at the same time in history and in the same location to carry out God's will. Similarly, our purpose is surrounded by the lives we are intertwined with daily and the lives we have an impact on daily.

Barak's fought hard in the war against the Canaanites, but he feared Sisera, and out of fear, he could not bring the war to an end. Nonetheless, Barak was willing to go. This shows us that if we have a willing heart, God can use all of us and will send us help when we need it. Just like Jael fixed Barak's lack of courage, God can use us in the same way. There are times, when like Jael, God will use our lives to rectify the mistakes and mishaps of other people. While we need to first turn our own mistakes into miracles of change, we may be called on by God to also fix the wrongs of other people. Let's go on this journey together as we strive to do more for God to have a positive impact.

God knew we all would make mistakes, lack courage or simply mess up. However, mistakes and circumstances can be turned around and can be used to help other people. As we will see in chapter one, we are placed on this Earth by design and in accordance to God's plan. We each have that choice to live out God's plan for our lives. When we choose to change our direction, and rise above mistakes, faults or circumstances, that is the first step. Jael gives us an example to take it to an even higher level. Allowing God to use us to turn the wrongs and mistakes of other people into miracles of positive change.

It is from us all working together unselfishly that we will see transformation and miracles.

To my family and friends from other faiths and perspectives, while I am in love with Jesus, we do have common ground. Our common ground is this, a deep love and respect for all human beings and this beautiful planet, and a need for courageous leaders, who put human dignity and care as their first priority. Like Jael, despite each other's backgrounds or faults, we can all come together and help our nation and our world. I present The Jael Effect, which is to turn mistakes into miracles!

PART I

WE ARE ALL A PART OF GOD'S PLAN

Being confident of this very thing, that He who has begun a good work in you will complete it until the day of Jesus Christ.

~Philippians 1:6

1 ~ BECAUSE OF WHO WE ALL ARE

So many of us are beaten down by mistakes that we have made. Some of us go on and on for years kicking ourselves and find it difficult to forgive the one person that we can never get away from, the person that looks back at us in the mirror. Some of us may be troubled by foolish acts that we may have done, and once we come to our senses, we ask ourselves, "Who was that person?" Others may be upset that they missed opportunities or relationships that they should have pursued. Then, there is this, "Why am I even here? Who gives a flip? It really will not make much difference if I am not here, maybe to my family and a few close friends, but that is about the extent of it." At one time or another, each of us has struggled with our mistakes, circumstances or faults. However, some of our faults and some of our mistakes are so grand that it impacts more than just our circle of people we come in contact with daily, but the entire world.

We experienced this in the midst of the COVID-19 Coronavirus and in the midst of the Black Lives Matter outcry for the acts committed against Black men and women. The mistakes or choices we make, and the impact of how far our mistakes can be felt, are evident. By the mere fact that there has been a worldwide outcry, let's us know that somebody somewhere messed up. People argue about whether or not the officers were right or wrong, but we are missing the point. Something is broken in how we are treating each other as human beings, and we need to come together to fix it. We have reacted or grieved as we witnessed the video showing four New York City police officers killing an unarmed Black man, Freddie Gray, as he cried out after being tackled to the ground, "I can't breathe."

In another video, we witnessed an incident on an evening in Texas when a police officer pulled over an unarmed African American woman, Sandra Bland, for not turning on her blinker as the officer forced her to the ground into handcuffs. Sandra cried out that he was hurting her arm, and later, she died while in police custody. Seeing the pain of these families, communities, and even the nation, imagine how this may have affected the consciousness of some of these officers. It is difficult to imagine that someone could even be so callous that rocking the very core of people's sense of humanity and decency would not be troublesome. We have to find a way to love and respect one another by treating everyone with dignity. God's Word tells us who we all are in Genesis 1:26-27 "Then God said, Let Us make man in Our image, according to Our

We are all a part of God's beautiful creation.

likeness…So God created man in His own image; in the image of God He created him; male and female He created them." We are all a part of God's beautiful creation.

In the meanwhile, in Georgia, an unarmed Black Man, Ahmaud Arbery, was out jogging in his lovely community, and three white men yelling racial slurs hunted him down hitting him with their truck and fatally shooting him in cold blood. In yet another incident in Kentucky, another Black family cried out as they learned that their daughter, Breonna Taylor, got killed while home sleeping in her bed by police officers, who stormed into her home looking for someone. Sadly, this was not even the correct address, and she was fatally shot.

These were just a few tragedies we witnessed before May 25, 2020, when the world watched a white police officer use his knee to pin an unarmed Black man face down to the street while he cried out with a bleeding nose, "I can't breathe."

These acts of violence are not just against Black people. They are crimes against humanity.

Two other police officers were holding him down and another standing with a gun between him and the crowd.

My heart was saddened once again as I watched the video of an unarmed Black man, Jacob Blake, get shot in the back at close range multiple times while getting into the car with his children by a white police officer. What is striking is that the officers did not care about the well-being of this man, his children in the car or any of the people watching. The truth is we just expect more from our leaders and the stewards over us. But let's be clear, violence is raging in America, and we are all at fault. In our cities, people are being gun down in the streets senselessly. These murders are resulting from a lack of resources, mental illness, lack of youth programs, dysfunctional homes, gangs, hatred and fear. As the human beings that God created and entrusted as stewards over His creation in Genesis 1:26-27, what are we doing to each other?

As the human beings that God created and entrusted as stewards over His creation in Genesis 1:26-27, what are we doing to each other?

Although all of the incidents involved acts of violence against Black people from authority figures, they have shaken up the entire world because racism and disregard for human life affects all of us. All of these tragedies put fresh faces on hate and the systemic racism of people of African descent in the United States and in other parts of the globe. All races continue to march in unity for justice because the inhumane treatment of one human being is a reflection on all of us. We need to learn from our mistakes and turn them around to create miracles to help all people. We need to understand that to elevate and lift up the least of us is to elevate and lift up all of us. Racism and hate is a mirror of the evil in humanity regardless of color. These acts of violence are not just crimes against Black people. They are crimes against humanity.

We need to respect the brave men and women who serve as police officers. The problem is not with all police officers. These men and women put their lives on the line to protect our streets. As with any other organization, we need to hold people accountable when they recklessly harm or kill other human beings. That is why we have laws. We need to have better screening of applicants, and ongoing and intense training and evaluations to weed out people and practices of bigotry and hate. Reform is needed on all levels to hold people accountability for reckless, harmful or fatal behavior towards other human beings. We know the abuse of authority and power is in every facet of our society. It is the job of every business and organization to hold people accountable and make it very clear that racism, bigotry and hate will not be tolerated. We all need each other!

Our Lives Are Interconnected

Our lives are interwoven with each other, which is captured in the African proverb, Ubuntu, which means, I am because we are. Ubuntu is from the Bantu language in Southern Africa explaining the relations that each of us has in connection with our community. As people in Korea, Australia, England, and countries throughout the world hold up Black Lives Matters' signs marching in the streets, we see the magnitude of our global community.

There is a universal bond of sharing that connects our humanity. In a very real sense, I would like to extend this Ubuntu sentence to, "I am who I am because of who we all are." Please allow me to take it to an even greater level for us all to understand that, "We are who we are because of who we all are." Maybe it takes away the scale of weighing whose purpose is the biggest; but instead, helps us to understand that we are all important. From the time of our birth to the time we leave this world, our very being affects everyone and everything around us.

Just like the environment which bred these white men in their thinking, it is possible that the pain, and the lost of Black lives could turn from tragedy to triumph for the cause of social justice. This would include miracles such as putting laws in place that hold all people and institutions accountable. We need miracles to bring about real reform so that all people feel valued and protected as well as more laws and actions to eradicate racism, such as every state having hate laws on the books. Good works are happening as people in all sectors of society find their voice in doing what they can to eradicate and break down systems of hate.

We Each Are A Piece Of The Puzzle

Each of us plays a role in this. We each make up one piece of a puzzle that is necessary for the completion of it. In understanding that, it is important to realize how each piece of the puzzle has its own standing with its own level of impact. The question is never about whether the puzzle piece has impact. Imagine God as the creator of the puzzle. When God created the puzzle, He made each piece of the puzzle to complete the picture in its finality.   This is the philosophy behind Ubuntu.

As a child of God, we were chosen to be a witness of God's love and goodness as He was laying down the Earth's foundations. What each of us does daily matters! God calls us to be a light. Even if we are hiding somewhere under a bushel, we are still impacting other people's lives. Since God has told us to let our light shine in the book of Mathew, if we have chosen not to, there is something missing in the lives of the people that we are supposed to be interwoven with daily.

The story about Jael has been one of my favorite Bible stories for years. Because when I read it initially, I thought, "Here is an ordinary woman, who was going about her daily life, and with her decision to be courageous and get involved,

15

she made an impact on an entire nation of people." Jael was engaged in life as a wife, a member of her community, and perhaps, as a mother, when suddenly her family had a visitor during wartime. No matter how ordinary we seem, I believe God has a plan for all of us to be courageous and get involved to make a difference in helping our nation.

Now, we have two philosophies with one application happening here. We have Ubuntu, and we have the Jael Effect. Here is the thought behind the Jael Effect; we each will make multiple impacts in the lives of those around us, and God in all of His sovereignly can still use us in a mighty way despite our mistakes; despite our faults and despite our circumstances. Some of our impact—both good and bad—will reach far out in the world. As we come to a deeper knowledge of the impact of our words and deeds, we can have a deeper appreciation for our lives and our interconnectedness as human beings.

Because of God's grace, we can turn our mistakes around for the good of others. We can turn our mistakes into miracles, which is The Jael Effect!

All of us as human beings make mistakes because it is a part of the human condition. We are not perfect beings. Yet, the Bible teaches us that God planned for our existence to serve him before the foundations of the world. Regardless of what

16

mistake we have made, there is redemption through Christ. Just as God has extended his grace to us, we need to accept his forgiveness and kindness, and in turn, extend grace to ourselves and to others. This is the first step. Because of God's grace, we can turn all of our mistakes around for the good of others. We can turn our mistakes into miracles, which is, The Jael Effect!

Our Human Ecosystem

To explain this further, let's examine the ecosystem, and how all of nature works together in balance because this is the same way that God has made human beings to work together in balance. In Florida, we had little lizards that crawled all over our house and yard. They were indeed a species that indicated that the environment was healthy in the neighborhood and that there were plenty of insects around to feed them. Another example of indicator species besides the little lizards are bees. Some scientists travel the world studying indicator species to monitor the environment's health by monitoring the numbers. For instance, in some areas, the number of bees, which pollinate the flowers are decreasing, which is of grave concern since we need them for pollination. God gave humans the responsibility of being stewards over His creation in Genesis 1:26. We need to do a better job in taking care of this beautiful planet that God made for us. We are all supposed to share, and take responsibility for the upkeep of our planet.

We are a part of a greater whole, and each life matters and is crucial to all of our survival and wellbeing.

We also need to do a better job in taking care of each other because the same is true with people. We need each other! We are a part of a greater whole, and each life matters and is crucial to all of our survival and wellbeing. We all make mistakes and are imperfect, but we are all valuable. It is a very subtle trend to devalue human life. It is happening right in front of our eyes as we witness firsthand the murder of George Floyd, Sandra Bland and Ahmaud Arbery. That needs to be of grave concern to all of us. If it was not obvious before, the COVID-19 World Pandemic will teach us all to value one another because all human life in whatever role each of us plays is critical for all of us and should not be taken for granted because we are each contributors to life on earth. In Genesis 1:26-27, God gave all human beings stewardship of the Earth.

Our Impact From Birth On

God planned our lives for this specific time and purpose to be a part of the ecosystem of human beings that are interconnected for this era. God created us knowing the details of our lives, such as, the family, place, or time frame of our birth. It was all part of His master plan. Our experience growing up could have a major impact on how successful we become and how fulfilled we feel in carrying out our dreams and aspirations. While many people thrive in spite of major challenges, others do not.

During the first quarter of our lives, the emotional fabric is laid out, and there are things that may happen that may haunt us for the rest of our lives. We can carry lifelong scars from harsh things like neglect, abuse, being bullied and feeling unloved. Sometimes, we may have scars that come from feeling jealous over a younger or older sibling being favored. Other times, we may have scars from feeling inferior because we felt we were not as smart, not as

Learning to let negative things and influences go is an essential step in turning misfortunes into miracles.

pretty or not as fast as other family members or friends. If this is the case, as we mature, we may need to work through any feeling stopping us from reaching our full potential. We may have to let some things go. Working through pain and letting negativity go in our lives helps us to be confident in reaching our greatest level of positive impact. Learning to let negative things and influences go is an essential step in turning misfortunes into miracles.

As I have worked with families around the country in different school systems as an educator and administrator, and with families in ministry as a former pastor's wife, it has become very evident that people of all ages are crying out for mentors, life coaches, or someone they can look up to for direction. Sometimes the impact we have in someone's life is simply being present. There is a need for godly people to embrace their experiences and realize that God has allowed us to go through all of our trials, tribulations, and victories. Oftentimes, this is what is necessary to earn the right to be heard. Surviving needs to graduate to thriving, and this needs to be celebrated. We also need to be comfortable in our own uniqueness. If we fail to embrace how valuable we are in our own uniqueness, we are teaching others that we influence not to value their own uniqueness. This may be our children or other people looking up to us. All of us need to embrace our diversity and differences as a beautiful part of God's creation.

Remember the words of the apostle Paul in First Corinthians 13:11, "Put away childish things..." In our early years, we may have a bouquet of both happy and sad experiences, but we have to purpose in our hearts, to embrace it all, and use it for God's glory. King Solomon said that there is nothing new under the sun, and if we are willing, God can use our experiences to speak encouraging words into somebody's life from the time we begin to speak, until our last breath.

Some Things Are Simply Not Fair

There are so many things that are simply unfair. One example of this may be our childhood since our early years in life are determined for us. The reality is that all of our beginnings are not created equal. In the book, *Outliers*, Malcolm Gladwell discusses how opportunity, timing and being in the right place at the right time in history gave way to the success of some of the world's most successful people.

Gladwell notes how expertise is derived through being able to practice a skill for at least ten thousand hours. Just think for a minute how different our life would have been and what we would think about yourself if you would have been born another color, black or white, rich or poor, in Zimbabwe or in Ireland, with only one arm or one leg. The Jael Effect of having an impact is even based on the premise that sometimes we have an impact simply because we were in the right place at the right time, surrounded by a preordained set of circumstances. Nonetheless, through our interconnectedness, our impact will be felt wherever our circumstances find us.

Gladwell gives numerous examples in *Outliers*, but one that I would like to note is that of the Rock group called the Beatles. Popular in the sixties, the Beatles came to the United

States and took Americans by storm. They were one of the most popular rock bands in recorded history. However, what many people may not know is the enormous practice that this group had in playing together. The Beatles played together for seven years before coming to America. They met a German Striptease Club owner in London, which had a domino effect of them meeting other striptease club owners. The striptease clubs were open every night, seven days a week with ongoing traffic. Thus, the Beatles moved to Hamburg, Germany, and played night after night nonstop.

This chance of being in the right place at the right time, to where the club owner just happened to meet them, and then, give them opportunity to play non-stop year after year, night after night, built expertise, which led to this band coming to America with their sound and their career taking off. The series of circumstances that led to the Beatles success can help us see the interconnectedness of our lives. Some things we control; some we do not control.

But there is a deeper lesson here that we need to consider. Do we really understand how some people have privileges that others may not have, and how that may have an impact? The Beatles had a lot of drive, but they also had a lot of opportunities to perform night after night. That opportunity may not have been given to someone else who had the same dreams of musical success. Perhaps they turned to a different path, perhaps it was meant for them to take that different path or perhaps not.

If we are not careful, we can forget that it is not just about us. It is about all of us, and how our choices can have an impact far beyond what we can see. Let's turn back a minute to the owners of the bars the Beatles used to perform in, do you really think those bar owners thought that one day those struggling artists who were performing in their bar were going to become international rock stars?

Our Impact Begets Impact

Many times our lives are bombarded with one point of view, and we succumb to that. The danger in this is that we miss the boat because we get tunnel vision, but God is omnipresent and omniscient. God may be asking us to open up our mental model and expand our thinking past our current lifestyle, current location, current people and current circumstances.

Many people arrogantly believe they've achieved success solely by their own efforts, but there are circumstances beyond our control that lends themselves to opportunity and privilege. I am reminded of the fact that people are limited by their physical abilities. Years ago, while working at a high school in New York, there was a very fine young man who we will call John. John worked extremely hard in school to pass his classes. All he wanted was to be able to serve his country in the military.

Sometimes what we want and what God wants doesn't match up, and as believers, we have to yield to God's plan. John had hurdles that he could not overcome due to his mental faculties. He had a low IQ and was considered mentally challenged. He wasn't able to pass the Regents exams, and even sadder, he wasn't able to get a high enough score on the ASVAB Military Entrance Exam. John was provided with accommodations in school and graduated with a Non-Regents diploma, which is a diploma awarded without passing the Regents exams.

There are many of us living through unfortunate situations. It may not always appear as if our lives are interconnected. Some mistakenly believe that some human lives don't matter because we often place value judgments on others based on superficial worldly standards and not God's standards. While John may not have been able to go in the military because of his IQ, God still had a grand plan for John's life. John turned his misfortune into a miracle. Imagine, after graduating from high school, John got a job, got married, and had a son, John, Jr., who became a doctor. John, Jr., saved hundreds of lives in the emergency room at their local hospital.

No life is worthless. John, Jr.'s, father was denied entry into the military because he was considered mildly mentally handicapped and couldn't pass the exam. However, he worked and supported his family, and he and his wife gave birth and raised a very gifted doctor. You see John, Sr., had no control over the mental capacity that he was born with or that he was not born even to a wealthy family. He did not start from a place of privilege. However, in spite of it, his life mattered, and his impact was enormous.

John, Jr., was able to have a father that was not traveling around in the military, but who provided a very stable life for him and who invested a lot of time in him. John, Jr., had a father who encouraged him and spent a lot of money making it possible for him to participate in science and math competitions and summer camps. John, Jr., did not achieve his success alone. The truth is that none of us achieves success by ourselves. To be wise is to know that it is by the sheer grace of God.

With miracles comes an understanding of how our outlook and attitude about our situation is an influencer of our direction, and the direction of our children. The Jael Effect can have an impact that last for generations.

Beyond his own choosing, John, Jr., was blessed to be in the home of loving parents, and to have a father, who encouraged and celebrated his son's intellectual capabilities. His father also nurtured, and helped him all the way through medical school. *"We are who we are because of who we all are."* We make an impact on each other's lives every single second of the day. In looking back at John, Sr., we see that with miracles comes an understanding of how our outlook and attitude about our situation is an influencer of our direction and the direction of our children. The Jael Effect is taking our circumstances and our situations, and choosing to get back up every time we fall. We each have to choose to live and finish strong, with whatever gifts, talents, and skills we have to carry out the plan that God has for us. John, Sr., exemplifies this! When we really think about it, at the end of the day, people will not care about our education; only the lives that we've touched. In looking back at John, Sr., we see that with miracles comes an understanding how our outlook and attitude about our situation is an influencer of our direction and the directions of our offspring. The Jael Effect can have an impact that can last for generations.

2 ~ CHANGE HAPPENS

Sometimes when God is calling you out for a purpose, it means that you have to come out of your comfort zone. This may mean that you need to form some new relationships with people who are different from you to connect with them for the tasks that God has put before you. I have experienced this in volunteering in African countries. When God wants to take us somewhere, it often will stretch us beyond our limits.

Years ago, when I first went to Africa for a humanitarian trip with Operation Crossroads, Africa, Inc. (OCA), we spent time in New York City before leaving from the John F. Kennedy International Airport. We traveled to London, England and enjoyed some time there, and had a brief stay in Frankfurt, Germany and Cairo, Egypt. Then, from Egypt, we traveled further into East Africa. We landed in Khartoum, Sudan, at one o'clock in the morning, their time. When I walked into the night air and saw my surroundings, none of the orientation I went through prepared me for the culture shock. It was one hundred degrees at one o'clock in the morning. I had to shake my head because I felt like I had landed on another planet. It was so hard for me to wrap my head around a place so different from America.

For the next two months living in Rosieres, Sudan, Africa, I was stretched to my limit. After settling into our routines, what started as a culture shock began to shift to a sense of familiarity with each passing day. The people so foreign to me became my friends, and I began to love them. This is why it is important to be brave enough to realize the world around us is interpreted by our point of view. In submitting to God's will for our lives, it will often bring about change, a new outlook on life. This is what Second Corinthians 5:17 is referring to when it says, "Therefore, if any man be in Christ, he is a new creature: old things are passed away; behold, all things are become new." While I adapted to and embraced the change and the people, what I thought was so strange at first, became my new normal. When we flew out of the country, I cried for having to leave my new friends. What is God asking of you that may be outside your comfort zone?

> *In submitting to God's will for our lives, it will often bring about a change, a new outlook on life.*

Guard Your Thoughts and Mind

God may not always be calling for us to move or go somewhere, but He may want to stretch us in other ways. Have you ever done something so stupid that it doesn't even matter if other people were mad at you because you were mad and angry with yourself? Years ago, I resigned from a job because I got tired of it. I beat myself up for allowing myself to get defeated and not persevere. It took some time, but I eventually forgave myself and moved on.

What I learned most from the experience is that Romans 8:28 is true. There are not any experiences that God cannot help us turn around for our good. This is why it is so important to understand that we cannot allow our past to control who we are or who we can become. We also cannot allow other people to define who we are or what we may become. It's imperative that we guard our minds. We must be careful of the negative impact others can potentially have in our lives.

There are people and forces that will purposely try to sabotage your thinking and your efforts. Some will do this through very tactical and strategic planning, and others will do it through their own hatred, bias and prejudices. You have to be mindful of your thought life to guard negative thinking, even from yourself. Forgive yourself, forgive others, and see yourself as God sees you. In Psalms 139:13 the Bible says, "For You formed my inward parts; You covered me in my mother's womb." This is letting us know that God knew and loved us even as we were forming in our mother's womb, and that we are all fearfully and wonderfully made. We have to let that rest in our souls to be able to forgive others and ourselves so that our mistakes can be transformed into miracles.

Don't Get Stuck

Not only do we need to learn from our mistakes and move forward, but also, in some cases, we may need to forget past success. If our past success is stopping us from living our personal best, then, we have to let go. You don't want to be that person always talking about what you did in high school or what you did in college because you are not satisfied with what you are doing now. What happened yesterday is gone, and God needs for you to live in the present for Him.

There are times when the best time of our lives were in the past, and when we look at our lives now, we just simply are not very happy. If that is you, don't settle for what your life used to be, and don't settle for what your reality may be today if you are not happy. Remember that the future is not here yet, and it may take a lot of work, but you can live your best life now. When I was growing up, the older saints in the church would sing, "I am so glad that trouble doesn't last always, ooooh, I am so glad that trouble doesn't last always...." Let the joy of the Lord be your strength, and continue to cry out to God asking for wisdom and guidance to see you through, which reminds me of another song, the older saints would sing, "...the storm is passing over, hallelujah."

We all will have our trials, but you can gain wisdom with each one. Through our varied experiences, we can learn invaluable lessons. The experiences that you have had gave you knowledge and experience that all of the books in the world could never replace. You felt it, smelled it, tasted it, heard it, survived it, and most of all, you lived through it firsthand. You are more than able to carry out God's purpose and plan for creating you. God has equipped you for what He has called you to do despite your past.

Speak Life to Yourself

The greatest voice in your mind is your own. It is crucial that we understand one of the most profound truths found in the Bible. Proverbs 23:7 tells us that "...as a man thinks in his heart, so is he." In other words, your self-talk will govern who you are and who you will become. People sometimes believe that if you talk to yourself, you're crazy. I'd argue that if your silent talk is not effective in making you a happier person in living your life to the fullest, then, you need to talk to yourself out loud quoting scriptures of affirmation, repeating positive quotes and saying positive words and phrases. God has a purpose and a plan for every phase of your life, and your life is interwoven with everyone around you. Remember, all that we go through is relative to our life's work or assignment.

God has a purpose and a plan for every phase of your life, and your life is interwoven with everyone around you.

In that conversation, tell yourself that you cannot look at other people and what they did or did not accomplish because the Creator gave you your own design and assignment. You can, however, look at other people as you work collaboratively with them in carrying out the work. For instance, as an educator, I have worked collaboratively with other educators in educating students. There are times when all of us have different tasks that we are supposed to do at different times in our lives, and the people we complete these tasks with will vary with the task we must accomplish.

It is important to digest this because as God works in our lives, we need to be able to let some people go, but just as important, we need to effectively work with and allow new people to come into our lives. This truth applies to our personal and professional life. Some people get stuck in a rut. We need to follow God's lead as He brings new people and new experiences into our circle. Sometimes God is calling us to move past what we are used to, but we meet Him with resistance, instead of simply yielding to His will.

Be Open to Change Zones

One day, while visiting with my Mom, we dined with a nice couple. We will call them Sheila and Dan. This couple embodied the concept of living your best life. Dan was sharing how he had enjoyed his career as a physicist, and then at the age of sixty, he went back to college to be a speech therapist. He talked about walking around campus and how the girls liked his mustache and so forth and so on. Five years later, his wife, Sheila, said, he walked across the stage with all of the young graduates and received his degree in speech therapy.

At this point, I thought about how nice it was that this senior citizen enjoyed going back to school. But that wasn't the end of the story. Dan got a job as a speech therapist and worked with children who needed speech therapy for five or six years. When we think of why we are here, there is no retirement from living out our purpose.

So I asked him, "Dan, which career did you like the best, the one as a physicist or the one as a speech therapist?" He said, "that being a physicist and being a speech therapist both reflected a different part of him and that both careers were endearing to him for different reasons." Dan's answer helped me to understand that in carrying out our purpose in life, we need to be in tune with our gifts, skills and talents because we, more often than not, have different assignments in fulfilling our life's purpose and work at different stages. From Dan's life and also the lives of the countless students he helped, it is important to note that with miracles, it sometimes involves a major change. Jael's life was changed forever. She went from obscurity to a nation's hero!

3 ~ YOU DON'T NEED ALL THE ANSWERS

As a parent, sometimes raising children gets so overwhelming as we juggle so many things. Other people who have raised children warn about how fast they grow up. Of course, we all want our children to become responsible adults, but the reality of us raising them coming to an end is not easy to accept. Yet, we watch as children in our lives transform into adulthood, and at some point, we have to let go for them to grow.

From about twenty to fifty, a lot of us are raising children and basically living out the prime of our lives learning as we go. Most of us are at the peak of our health, vitality and strength. However busy or active, successful or unsuccessful, this time may be, we look up one day, and the next thing we know, this period of our life is over. It seems the rat race and hustle of working, raising children, attending social functions, going to worship, supporting school programs, sports teams and taking care of the house, will always be. But moving into the next phase, the children are not children anymore. Most will become the independent adults you raised them to be, living their own lives and managing their own affairs. This can bring about a sense of emptiness, uncertainness and uneasiness.

As we transition into the next phrase, some of us were wise and prepared. Some are able to retire with their spouse, date again and travel the world. Some simply enjoy a quiet and happy life loving on the grandkids and laughing together. However, moving into this time in our lives may bring other types of experiences and emotions. Maybe some of us aren't married, and as we grow older, we wonder if it will ever happen for us. Some of us may just have given up on the idea of marriage or simply decided it is not something we want. We just may find ourselves in unusual situations, and whether we are married, single, divorced or widowed in this season, this may be a little scary.

What if you did everything you planned to do, and somehow things did not quite go as planned? Circumstances and fate forgot to consult you and get your permission to turn your plans around. That spouse who you thought would be there forever is gone. The reasons behind why they are gone may vary. Perhaps it is from separation due to sickness, divorce, or death. On top of that, the kids had the nerve to grow up, and more times than not, they may have even moved out of town.

One scripture that I think about all the time is this, "It is appointed unto men once to die and after this the judgment." (Hebrews 9:27) Now, to some this scripture may sound a bit morbid, but it is a very important reminder that we are not promised tomorrow. We only have now, literally, right now. The gift of today is today. You are living your life today, right now.

This realization first came to me at a young age when I was in middle school. I had a minor surgery and was out of school for about a week. Before that, I had a classmate that I love to play around with in class. He was the cutest little brown haired white boy, and we used to like to blow spitballs (tiny rolled up paper) and crack jokes. When I got out of the hospital and went back to class, I started looking for my little buddy, and I asked about his whereabouts. I was shocked to find out that he was hit by a car and died.

All of a sudden, the realization that I was not too young to die hit me. Wherever you are in your life, get busy living your best life because you are not promised to make it to a ripe old age. The reality in all of this is that for any of us, our last tomorrow may be today. Be grateful for today, live. None of us have all the answers. We are all trying to learn to navigate through life as we go.

Having More Than One Purpose

As we move through the different stages in our life our main purpose may change. In understanding how we often have multiple purposes in our life that God needs us to fulfill, I am reminded of a young engineer, who we will call Gloria.

Gloria travelled on a mission's trip that I led while I was at New Song Bible Fellowship Church in Lanham, Maryland.

Gloria started working as an engineer fresh out of college, and after working in the profession for eleven years, she believed that God had something more for her to do and wanted to go on a mission trip to seek God's will for her life. While in Ghana, we partnered with a mission's agency there who had a handsome leader that worked with us. Let's call him Tom. Before surrendering to full-time Christian service, Tom had received a college education, was fluent in French, and on his way to becoming an ambassador for his country. But God had other plans for Tom, and he planned to go to Bible College and become a missionary in Northern Africa.

The day before we left to return back to America, Tom said to me, "When you go back to America, look after Gloria for me." Suspecting the obvious, I said to him, "Tom, if you want someone to look after Gloria, you will have to do it yourself." Tom went on to tell me that he was romantically interested in Gloria. I told him that we were leaving tomorrow, and it would be okay if he wanted to let Gloria know, and he did. Initially, I had my concerns of his intentions. However, God blessed this relationship, and the two of them found their way back together, married, had children and went on to serve God in ministry.

It is amazing to watch God at work. Gloria felt in her heart that God had something different for her besides working as an engineer. She had taken vacation leave from her job to go on the mission's trip to Ghana, West Africa, and she was open to what God had for her life. This was all in God's perfect timing, and He brought Tom into her life so they could fulfill their destiny together. At the age of thirty-two, they both had their lives changed forever, but this would have never happened if they both had not been open to what God had for them.

Fulfilling The Promise

Today is the day to chart your course with a vengeance. The people that are the happiest are the people who are doing what they were born to do. While writing this book, I worked as an administrator in a public school. I had lived and travelled in different parts of the world and was busy trying to serve God by serving people. Yet, something in me was thirsting for more.

We see over and over in the Bible how people served God until they were physically unable to serve him any longer. Essentially, whatever assignment you may need to complete, God can use the knowledge gained from your life's story as you trust Him for where He is taking you. So many of us are looking online, at social media, magazines and television for our information and are losing sight of what is real. You are real, and your life is interwoven and being felt by the people who are around you daily. *"We are who we are because of who we all are."*

There are times when we may have missed one of God's assignments, or perhaps it was simply not time yet. This will leave a burning within you for something you want to do or accomplish. Psalms 37:4-6 speaks to us in saying, "Delight yourself also in the Lord, and He shall give you the desires of your heart, commit your way to the Lord, trust in Him, and He shall bring it to pass. He shall bring forth your righteousness as the light, and your justice as the noonday."

God has a plan for our desires because the Word is clear. Psalms 37:23 tells us that, "The steps of a good person are ordered by the Lord and that God delights in the way." In short, God has a purpose and a plan for our lives in every season, and in finding Him, we can live out the purposes for which we were created until our last day here on this Earth. It is not so cut and dry that we only have one purpose. God can have several purposes or assignments for us to complete, and He gives us talents and abilities accordingly. We need to celebrate the positive impact we have had on the people around us. We all need each other.

Remember, Jael was just an ordinary person going about her day-to-day routines with her family. However, in just a moment, her impact with one deliberate decision changed the course of war in bringing forth a victory for the Israelites. It landed her name in the greatest book and the number one bestseller of all time, the Bible.

Consider this, in chapters twelve through twenty of Genesis, God repeatedly promised Abraham that he would give him a son and bless his descendants mightily. Watching the years go by, Abraham and Sarah looked at their aging older bodies, and they doubted God at His word. Finally, they did what we all do time and time again. They took matters into their own hands.

Immediately, there was strife between the two women, and Abraham gave Sarah the liberty to deal with Hagar however she wished. Thus, Hagar and Ishmael were driven out of the compound. We all have made so many mistakes in our lives. Yet, despite our faults, God has helped us, blessed us and even used us for a purpose. Just think about how many times you may have messed up, and God still worked it all out for you. In this story about Abraham and Sarah, there is a promise of redemption for every human being who has ever made a mistake, taken the wrong turn, or simply disobeyed God.

God promised them clearly that He would bless them with an heir through Sarah. They should not have forced Hagar to have sex with Abraham for him to get an heir. They sinned against God by not believing and trusting in His promise to them, and not to mention, by Abraham committing adultery with Hagar. However, God can work through with our lives, even with all of our mistakes. He can work with our mess-ups and turn them into miracles. The reason being, He is God!

Over and over again, God reinforced His promise to Abraham and Sarah. God said that He would bless and multiply Abraham's seed, and that all the nations of the earth would be blessed through his seed. Genesis 21:1-2, "And the Lord visited Sarah as He (God) had said, and the Lord did for Sarah as He had spoken. For Sarah conceived and bore Abraham a son in his old age, at the set time of which God had spoken to him." The lessons we can learn from this is that God never goes against His Word. What God says He will do, He will do.

God can work with our mess-ups and turn them into miracles. The reason being, He is God!

Next, notice the scripture tells us that "at the set time" God acted. Every single act is in accordance to God's timing. There was a line in a song that we used to sing growing up, "He may not come when you want Him, but He is right on time." Nothing happens unless God allows it to be so, which is why we need to be very careful in disobeying God because He has given us free will, and we don't really want God to just leave us to our own devices without divine help.

We are a world of individuals who have free will to influence and impact other individuals collectively. May I just add here that the Holocaust was God leaving mankind to his own devices. The sex trafficking and enslavement of human beings worldwide is God leaving mankind to his own devices. The racism, mass incarceration, selfishness and the social injustices that we are witnessing around the globe are examples of God leaving mankind to his own devices. In our fighting and killing one another, this is God leaving mankind to his own devices.

Getting back to the story, we also see with Abraham and Sarah that God can work around our lives even when we mess up. We are human beings, and God knows we are going to make mistakes. But if we repent and get our focus back on God, the Lord will give us the power and ability to work around, through, over and under our mistakes and carry out His purpose and plan for our lives.

We Are Not New to God

Solomon said it best in Ecclesiastes 1: 9, "That which has been is what will be, that which is done is what will be done, and there is nothing new under the sun." Solomon doesn't even stop there, in verse 10, he said, "Is there anything of which it may be said, "See, this is new? It has already been in ancient times before us." In gist, the type of person that we are, and the mistakes that we have made, are not new to God.

We have to be all so careful in western culture of the liberties we have to freely express ourselves. As believers, we are still to surrender our lives as a testimony for God's glory, not our own. We have to be careful not to get caught up in our problems either. For example, in posting on social media, we need to check ourselves to make sure our pictures are not edifying ourselves, but our creator. Even though it is popular to post selfies and pictures all over social media, we have to ask ourselves, "What is the purpose?" and "Who are we edifying?" Most of us love it! There is no shame or limit to how much we can share, but in all of our sharing, we need to glorify our Savior. Good or bad, in Ephesians 1:21, teaches us that everything about us should be used as a testimony of Christ's grace and mercy because our goal should be to live our best for Him. While we may be special in our individuality, there have been many types to resemble us in history.

King Solomon goes on to say in verse 11, "There is no remembrance of former things, or will there be any remembrance of things that are to come by those who will come after." In short, the world has a short history, and there is a time and a season for everything. If you recall, earlier we discussed how none of us chose when, where or to whom we would be born, and we are all important and our lives are interwoven. Remember, Ubuntu? I am who I am because of who we all are. "*We are who we are because of who we all are.*" We discussed how the Earth has an ecosystem where all things work together.

There should not need to be a global outcry over the racism, injustices and violence being committed against people of African descent worldwide. This is not only a result of hate, but also a result of a lack of understanding. The Word of God teaches us in 1 John 3:15, that, "Whoever hates his brother is a murderer, and you know that no murderer has eternal life abiding in him." From the very beginning of the Bible in Genesis 1:26-27, we learn that we are all made in the image and likeness of God, and Roman 2:11 teaches us that there is not any partiality with God. The need for one individual to place their worth over another individual or for one group of people to place their worth over another group of people is not biblical. It is mean and ungodly. Every human life is essential and matters, and we are all contributors on earth. Is it any wonder that many people with ill intentions and hate want to misquote or disregard the Bible, which is clear in God's value for all human beings?

God needs for us to be in tune with Him because He is the Author and Finisher of the Earth and of all time. God needs for us to allow Him to work around our mistakes and carry out the purposes and plan for which we were created in every season of our lives and at this time in human history. From the life of Abraham and Sarah, we can clearly see that God will forgive anybody. God will help us to turn our lives around and use that which is not favorable, and turn it into, not just good, but greatness.

God will help us to turn our lives around and use that which is not favorable, and turn it into, not just good, but greatness!

4 ~ WHETHER MARRIED OR SINGLE

We need to embrace where we are. Jael simply did what needed to be done right there in her tent. Our society breeds on us being unhappy or discontent. We may have been feeling perfectly fine about our lives until we started looking at some programs, commercials or advertisements, which were designed to have us start the comparison game. Oh, well my hair doesn't look like that, or my stomach, or my chest, or my legs...don't look like this. We all need to stop. When we are married, we dream of being single. When we are single, we dream of being married. How about we choose to be happy just the way we are, wherever we are. But let's talk more about being married and single, and may I add here that when the Israelites sing praises to Jael for their miracle, do you think it mattered if she was single or married?

Paul says to us in Philippians 4:11-13, "Not that I speak in regard to need, for I have learned in whatever state I am, to be content. I know how to be abased, and I know how to abound. Everywhere and in all things I have learned both to be full and to be hungry, both to abound and to suffer need. I can do all things through Christ who strengthens me." In whatever situation we are in, we can be strengthened through Christ. Praise in the joyful times and praise through the pain.

In all, like the old saints at my church used to say growing up, "praise God anyhow!" In other words, don't let your circumstances steal your joy or determine how much you praise God. Regardless of what you are going through, praise God anyhow! But let's talk about marriage for a minute because it has been a vital part of our journey. Marriage is a part of everyone's life in one way or another, whether it is yours or someone else's marriage. We are all affected by marriage. Couples sometimes get so wrapped up in life and its problems that they lose each other. Many of these couples eventually only tolerate each other and grow apart, but it doesn't have to be that way.

Let's go back a little. My family moved to a nicer community in Adelphi, Maryland when I was in high school around seventeen years old. We were like the old TV show, The Jeffersons. We moved up as my parents could do better. We moved into a split- level house with a finished basement, except the laundry room. In the finished portion, there was the possibility for two bedrooms, but one area needed a wall with a door to make it just right. That would be my room. For the first time in my life, I would have my very own bedroom. Outside of my room was the family room, which had a fireplace. How I loved that fireplace in the winter.

I would sit and stare at the fire for hours, but there was a trick to keeping it going. One, if you didn't remember to open the damper, the smoke from the fire would back into the house. But that wasn't enough. In order for the fire to burn endlessly, you had to keep adding logs, and then, it would burn for hours and hours. Such can be said with marriage. If you want to keep the fire in your marriage burning, you have to keep throwing logs on it. These logs consist of loving, gifts, dates, good lovemaking, and lots and hugs and kisses.

Staying Married

Marriage is a decision everyday to say I do. When you stop making that decision, the marriage is in trouble. If you are blessed with a good mate, purpose in your heart together to say, "I do" everyday, and then, put a log on the fire of your marriage, the flames keep burning. A log that is needed daily is loyalty because what happens in many marriages is not a lack of love, but a lack of loyalty. When couples are dating and in love, they are loyal to each other, and it seems the world stops and time stops. All of a sudden, nothing is more important than the person you love, and you make time and find ways to be with each other.

Couples take the oath believing their love is enough, but as equally important is loyalty. This trust of loyalty is often broken when life happens, and the loyalty is compromised. Loyalty may be compromised by a job, friends, ministry, church, hobbies, children or a family member that a spouse may put in front of the person that once held the position as the center of their life. In a successful marriage, loyalty cannot be compromised. If you want your marriage to prosper and flourish, your spouse must always be your first priority, and then, together you conquer the world. No matter what happens, keep each other first, have each other's back, and do life together. This is the beauty of having a companion. God should be the center of your relationship. Marriage is ordained in the Bible starting with Adam and Eve.

Appreciate Your Position, Single or Married

It is so important for married people to respect singleness and single people to respect marriage. Focus on the good of both and relish where you are in your life. As a married woman, my husband and I had some great times with our children. I appreciated being married and raising a family. Some marriages are made in Heaven, and the couple seems to work together seamlessly. But other marriages have unspeakable trials and tribulations. In my marriage, we encountered a lot of obstacles and somehow we lost our way and forgot to put the logs on the fire. Our loyalty was compromised as we put other things in front of each other. The fact of the matter is this, sometimes in putting the logs on the fire, you have to crawl with every ounce of strength you have. Other times, you need outside friends to help you carry the logs. If you are married and want to stay married, whichever applies, do it!

I render my story merely as a lesson for whoever can use it. Marriage is an institution made by God. Even though you may have failed in a previous marriage or marriages, and even though some people's marriages around you are in trouble, don't fault the institution. We must simply learn from each other's mistakes and find joy in our own lives. If married, remember to open the damper to the chimney by allowing the Holy Spirit to come in and help you to forgive each other, help you to respect each other and help you to love each other. Put the logs on the fire of your marriage everyday by saying I do and give each other "first" priority over everything but God.

Establish Marriage Negotiations

You may also need to put on a log on the fire of your marriage by re-negotiating. What happens in a lot of our marriages is that we get married with one set of rules and ideas, and years past, and then, we change after maturing. I used to have a job in Alternative Education where we established Cooperative Agreements with different agencies that we worked with to service the particular needs of students. We would negotiate the relationship norms and revise as needed before signing off every two-years. Why couldn't we apply the same principle to our marriage? Some marriage counselors and pastors are poorly trained, and couples go through counseling seeking guidance and the marriage still ends in divorce. That is pretty poor counseling results. Let's consider this, in business we think logically and use experience and knowledge in negotiating to handle our affairs. Oftentimes, in our relationships, we don't use any of this knowledge, but act out of sheer emotions.

If two people are committed to loving each other and working together, planned negotiation meetings may be needed to make sure the correct logs are being thrown on the fire. Some couples can do it themselves, but it is important to have open conversations to renegotiate and review a marriage Cooperative Agreement to avoid ever having to review a divorce agreement. In doing this, there has to be transparency and honesty. Both parties must have a desire to commit to this process. Think outside of the box, but inside the Word of God, and do what is necessary to make your marriage work. Establish your non-negotiables, and then go from there in creating your Marriage Cooperative Agreement.

Being Single

Being single after a divorce or the death of a spouse calls for you to rethink the priorities in your life. Everything that you were as a couple calls for reevaluation. For both women and men, it is a major adjustment when you are no longer a husband or wife. For singles who have never been married, it is typically assumed that you want to get married, and more often than not, pressure is put on you to find a spouse. One of the single retreats that I attended had a theme called "Diamond in the Rough." The idea behind it was that the singles attending were diamonds in the rough being developed for marriage. The truth is people are single for various reasons. In fact, some people will never marry because their purpose and assignments that God has for them will work best if they remain single, and that is okay.

We started in this chapter discussing how it is so important that we don't spend our lives being discontent or always thinking the grass is greener on the other side. What would happen if we just decided to get busy loving God and carrying out our assignments from Him right where we are and trust God's sovereignty to use our situations?

The Bible instructs us in Philippians 4:11, to be content in whatever state we find ourselves in. The Bible is not saying this for us to stagnate in growing as a human being, but rather, this verse is saying that we need not let our circumstances determine the outcomes of our lives or determine whether or not we have joy. We can be content because we know that the Holy Spirit of God is working in us wherever we find ourselves. According Philippians 2:13, this is to His will and His good pleasure.

There are times and events that make us so happy. But true joy is from God, and He gives it in abundance to anyone, anywhere, and at any stage in life, whether single or married, rich or poor. God has a purpose and a plan for everyone's life. Knowing that the Creator of the universe loves us and made us on purpose to be a part of a greater whole should be enough. In terms of knowing who we are, *"we are who we are because of who we all are."* God has assignments for all of us to complete during our time here on Earth before He calls us home to be with Him.

In remembering my life verse, "But seek ye first the kingdom of God, and His righteousness and all these things shall be added unto you." (Matthew 6:33). Somehow that verse had a whole new meaning as I pondered over the later part of that verse, "all these things." When we move from our mistakes to miracles, the "all these things" from this verse involves the transformation of miracles happening within our lives.

5 ~ OUR GOD HAS A PLAN

We all can be impactful and used at any age. Sometimes students will dare to ask us educators our age. This is an opportunity for a teachable moment. So I explain to them why they shouldn't ask a woman her age. We have explored some things about the different stages in our lives, but let's talk even more openly about age. Some people will tell you that once they start getting a little age on them that they feel more confident about who they are, more so than ever before. Maybe it is just that you are wise enough to know, things that used to matter aren't even important anymore. But that is not with everyone, some people regret getting older and start stressing over what they did or didn't do.

As we age and move through our lives, we gain knowledge and experience. With each passing year, our life experiences may or may not be valued by the world, but they are valuable to God because He wants to use our experiences for His glory. People in the Bible served God from their youth until their last breath and were revered for their wisdom and knowledge. God can use anyone who has the wisdom at any age to serve people for the good of humanity. We are never too young or too old to serve. That is not to say that we should not retire from our jobs when you want, whether in religious or secular work. The point is that God can use any of us, regardless of age, and we need to keep on serving God until the end of our lives and realize our immense value to Him.

In Moving Forward

It is important to not get caught up with negativity. Paul puts it this way in Philippians 3:13, "Brethren, I count not myself to have apprehended: but this one thing I do, forgetting those things which are behind, and reaching forth to those things, which are ahead." We have to let some things go.

Sometimes it is easy to get discouraged because we can think about all the things we wanted to do. This is faulty thinking because it is never too late to do anything if it is in God's will for our lives. So while there may be some things that are weighing us down that we simply have to let go, there are other things that we may have in the palm of our hands that God wants us to use. He planned out our life from beginning to end.

Until we breathe our last breath, God has a purpose for us being here on this Earth. God wants to use our life as a light and blessing to other people.

Consider Philippians 1:6 KJV, "Being confident of this very thing, that he which hath begun a good work in you will perform it until the day of Jesus Christ." In other words, until we breathe our last breath, God has a purpose for us being here on this Earth. God wants to use our life as a light and blessing to other people in doing His work until we meet Him.

Experiences Are Invaluable

God has encouraging words for you to tell somebody. There are people rising up in your shadow that need to know what you have learned in your journey, and you have earned the right to be heard because you have survived it and experienced it. In other words, you have lived it! Remember, the principles of Ubuntu. I am who I am because of who we all are. Sharing may mean coming out of your comfort zone and being vulnerable. But listen to this, no one can tell your story better than you, and you don't know how people will connect or be moved as a result of you telling it. There are people that God wants to touch through you because there is something about you they can connect with.

You know all of us have different professions, careers and circumstances, and our paths are distinctly ours. It is our story for God to use for our sphere of influence. He placed us in this time and space. It may be to simply raise an awesome human being. What else is Jesus' mother known for? It doesn't even matter if you are in full-time Christian work or in secular work. God has His people stationed everywhere. In fact, all believers are in Christian work, and wherever God has placed us, we are to be ambassadors for Him. The Bible is clear in that it teaches us that, "Whatever we do, we are to do as if you are doing it for the Lord and not as if you are doing it for men." (Colossians 3:33)

Using All Your Gifts

The time to determine what other areas of growth is needed is now. It is time to expand more than we have ever expanded before to lift up the Name of Jesus. We need to be open to allow God to use all that He put in us. You don't need the strength of your youth nor do you need to be a certain age. Every single person in this world was created with a gift or talent to use at any age, young or old. The Bible teaches us, in First Corinthians 12, that everyone has a gift. Many believers have shared their gifts in different ways and in different places, but I want to venture to say that there are hundreds of believers that are holding on to a gift that God gave them. For whatever reason, they are simply not using it. First Corinthians 12:4 tells us, "Now there are diversities of gifts, but the same spirit." What we can learn from this is that God created us all with many different abilities for us to work together for His glory.

The Bible validates itself, and the message is clear from the Old Testament in Psalms 139:4, which lets us know that we are fearfully and wonderfully made, to the New Testament, which lets us know that we all have talents that we are supposed to use. Of all that God created here on this Earth, there is nothing more precious to Him and that should be more precious to us than human life. God teaches us in Hebrews 2:7 that we were all made a little lower than the angels. In First John 4:20, it let's us know that our love for God is only evident in the love we have for each

Our love for God is only evident in the love we have for each other.

other. The plan that God has for us may not always be obvious or make a lot of sense, but God created everything and everyone for a purpose and that every human life is of great value to Him. He gives each of us talents and gifts to use in carrying out His plan.

In a parable in the twenty-fifth chapter of Matthew, Jesus talks about the rich man that gave all of his servants a talent, and each servant used his talent in a different way, except the one servant that did not do anything. This servant held on to his talent because he thought the rich man was stingy and wouldn't give him anymore. This, of course, offended the rich man. While this parable may be showing us how God gives us talents and that we shouldn't be like the servant and not use them, there is still hope.

Some of us have other reasons for holding on to our talents; some reasons unforeseen, some foreseen. But the thing to consider is that time is short, and the world and circumstances can change in an instance. If you are the servant who is still holding on to your talent, and in your heart, you know that God has given you a certain talent or gift, now is the time. God is not like the rich man. You may still have time to do all that He asks of you for Him. You are still here. Even if you are in pain, your time is not up. Don't let the troubles of this world stop you.

The aftermath of my divorce was almost like losing a spouse to death. It was the death of a union. When I was going through it, especially after being married for so many years, my heart was broken in two. Working in such a demanding profession, I didn't have much time to grieve. Once we separated, I knew I still had talents that God put in my hand, but now I was on my own to use them. This was a strange time for me because when I was married, outside of my job, I used all of my talents to help him in church ministry. When we go through life's troubles, it doesn't change the fact that God created us intentionally and planned for us. What we experience doesn't change the fact that we have talents and gifts that we have been equipped with in living out our purpose in living for Christ.

It is amazing how some of the most gifted people endure the most troubles and are the most overlooked. Sometimes people's talents are hidden by a physical or mental handicap, or drugs, violence, depression, poverty, poor decision-making, or sometimes, it seems it is just plain bad luck. It is what we tell ourselves in our self-talk that determines who we are now and what we will do tomorrow. Everyone falls, but when you fall, get back up, every time!

Appreciate Your Journey's Impact

Problems only give us more knowledge, more depth and make us stronger to withstand trials. After years of living and ministering in different places in the world, what I learned about people of all races and backgrounds is that there is so much value in who we are, and what we tell ourselves about our own stories impacts who we think we are. In fact, one of our greatest problems is that we don't understand that what we do does not give us worth. Our worth is an inherited gift from our Creator who made humans a little lower than the angels to have dominion over Earth. God thinks we are all pretty special. He thinks we are so special that He offered Himself as a sacrifice for all of mankind.

Our worth is an inherited gift from our Creator who made humans a little lower than the angels to have dominion over the Earth.

Years ago, my ex-husband and I started a church in Mississippi, and being that my father was a pastor and started a church in Washington, D.C., my mom encouraged me to keep taking piano lessons to play hymns for the church. So I grew up playing the piano, and singing in choirs at church and school. I suppose by most people's standards I was a well-qualified first lady. The truth is all that was in me was being poured out in my job as a school teacher and as a pastor's wife, unofficial assistant pastor, pianist, ladies' ministry director, Sunday School teacher, youth leader, mother, student and a school teacher.

While working as a teacher and serving in ministry for eight years in Mississippi, God blessed me with two children. From Mississippi, God used us to minister in different places. Now, I could give you more intricate details of life in all of these places, but I would get to writing about the snow in Syracuse and how I thought I was in the North Pole, or the Mississippi heat being hotter than the heat in Gambia, West Africa, when I lived there. So I will not get sidetracked. We are talking about how our journeys may all be different, and all of us may have different paths, but understanding our worth and impact in the world is crucial. God made us all, and it is uncanny how similar we are and how vital we are to one another's existence.

After moving to Florida, our marital journey came to a slow and dying halt. So while I was going through the death of my marriage, God gave birth to a new organization tying my two great loves and two gifts together, education and international service. It seems like God whispered in my spirit; I am not through with you. Now you are on your own and can still use all that I put in you. It is amazing how God can take something hurtful or something broken and turn it around. Maybe that is the essence of Roman 8:28, which tells us that all things work together for good to those who love God and to those who are called according to His purpose. All of our life's lessons can be used for a positive impact.

6 ~GOD WILL BRING IT ALL TOGETHER

Sometimes, we just need to trust God to do His work in our lives. When I was in my teens, I didn't want to share my room with one of my cousins when she came to live with us while attending college. I had just gotten my own room. This was my parent's idea. I wanted her to stay in the guest room upstairs next to their room, but my parents wanted us teens downstairs. Now that I've raised two teenagers, I understand why. At the time, I didn't see the plan God had for me.

My cousin spent her junior year in high school living in Kenya, East Africa. While living in my room, she told me about her experiences in Kenya. Out of her mouth and into my life, she helped me to develop a global vision. Matthew 6:33 has guided my life for over forty years, and at various stages and situations, it has guided me in different ways. For instance, the verse says that if we seek God, then, "all things would be added unto us." Oftentimes, the assumption is that "all things" are limited to tangible physical objects. However, "all things" depends on your circumstances because there are times that "all things" may be safety and peace. This was exactly what I needed throughout my humanitarian work in The Gambia, West Africa.

Ten years after volunteering the first time in Sudan, I went back to Africa with Operations Crossroads Africa out of as a team leader for a building project in The Gambia, in West Africa. The villagers provided us with potato sacks filled with straw and a compound with a three-room building not too far from the water well. The guys slept in one room, and the ladies in the other, with a curtain separating us. The village did not have running water, but the third room had a tub where we fetched water from the well and took bucket baths.

The compound did not have plumbing for toilets, but we did have an outside area with a latrine. The hole that was created for the latrine was kept clean, and we all knew when the curtain was closed, someone was handling business. We had brought our sleeping bags and mosquito nets, and so we sat up our bed areas using the potato sacks as our mattresses. We were grateful for their hospitality in creating this place for us to be a part of their community.

Our village did not have electricity but was nicely organized with clean dirt roads and nice forest surrounding it; one of which led to a neighboring village where my co-African group leader's family lived. OCA teamed with an organization in the Gambia called the President's Award's Scheme. My co-leader led a team of about seven Gambians, who lived and travelled with my team of seven. This was great for these young people because they were all studying and preparing for their future as well as the college and graduate students on my team from America. At any rate, the closest town to our village was five kilometers away, and we would take an older van, serving as public transportation into town. The van would run throughout the day. We had a tight budget so renting our own van and driver was out of the question. All of our money needed to be used to buy the supplies for the project, and in addition to that, I had to buy groceries, hire a cook and feed everyone. I never knew so many people could fit into a van, but between the public vans and taxis, my team and I travelled all over The Gambia and Senegal.

After being in The Gambia for about a month, I woke up early, as usual, to have my devotion on the bench outside in our compound. I loved the fresh and cool early morning air, the melodies of the birds and chickens, and watching the children come onto our compound to gather fruit off the mango tree. Eventually, people throughout the village, including my team, would wake up, and the public van would begin its runs for the day.

During the week, we would work on the building, and on the weekend, we would have fun sightseeing or going to the beach. Yes, in case you don't know, Africa not only has beautiful beaches, but it has beautiful and luxurious resorts. It is a popular tourist spot and not just for the exotic animals. Anyway, back to the story, on one particular weekend, I had a special treat for my team, and we were all looking forward to it. While in the Gambia, we visited the America Embassy and American clubs a few times to stay in touch. We had heard that an American naval ship was coming to the Gambia, and I remember thinking how great that would be for the team to get an "American fix." It's funny—when we were in a foreign non-western country far, far from home, hamburgers and French fries never looked so good.

But on this particular Saturday, when I went out to sit on the bench for my quiet time, there were not any people walking around nor were there any people waiting for the van to go into town. The village was totally quiet. Finally, when the team woke up, we were all stunned to find out from my co-leader's transistor radio that there had been a coup. A young military general by the name of Yahya Jammeh ousted a long term standing president named Sir Dawda Jawara, and the American naval ship we were going to visit, left carrying the ousted President. For the next week, the entire country was shut down on curfew with no phone service, transportation—nothing. To eat, everyday we had to walk five kilometers to town to buy fresh groceries or food from wherever we could find open vendors. Remember, we had no electricity, which meant we did not have refrigeration. However, we learned some things about how to store certain food by burying it in the ground and so on. After the coup, the entire country was quiet from being on lockdown. Needless to say, I had a few team members that were worried.

Nonetheless, The Gambia was and still is a peace-loving country, and the people were ready for a change because despite the severity of the situation, the coup was bloodless. There was not any resistance from the people. It was a military takeover, and there were mean-looking soldiers parading through the streets holding up their guns everywhere. After about a week, we were allowed to go back to life as usual, and public transportation started up again. Businesses opened back up. People began to fill the streets again, and the phone service was turned back on. Our families were horrified back in the United States. After the phones came back on, we all called home and assured everyone that we were fine.

Being that I grew up in Maryland outside of Washington, D.C., my family had ties all over the city, and you better believe they were calling everybody working their way right up to the White House. I had assured my family and my team that everything was going to be alright. This was despite the fact that we had to go through checkpoints throughout our travels by being searched by armed military soldiers at gunpoint, and the fact that the United States Embassy was strongly suggesting that we leave The Gambia immediately. God had already given me peace that we were all going to go back home safe and sound. Philippians 2:13, "For it is God which works in you both to will and to do of his good pleasure." For the believer, man never has the last Word, God does.

During this time, my life verse, "But seek ye first the Kingdom of God and His righteousness, and all these things shall be added unto you," meant that while I was serving in The Gambia and taking care of my team of seven in conjunction with my African partners, God's "all these things" was safety, protection, good health and a peace of mind. So often, we equate God's provisions and blessings with wealth or material possessions, but these things sometimes come at a great price, and sometimes it is not what you need.

While stranded in a country that had shut down all communication, land and sea transportation, and airports, God took care of our physical needs. Officials at the U.S. Embassy told me that at least they felt comfort in that we were living out in the bush since most of the military action was in town. But the God that I served provided for us during those final weeks as we came to the end of our summer assignment and travelled through the Gambia making our way back to Senegal to catch our return flight. Even though we were stopped and searched at checkpoints until we got into Senegal, not one inch of our bodies or one hair strand on our head was harmed. God provided us with safety, protection, good health and peace of mind.

Sometimes You Have To Seek Him

As I embarked on writing this book, I had been asking God to give me direction. I didn't want to just be satisfied in living my present life, and just settle in that, or reminisce about my past, both the good, great and not so great. I wanted to make sure I didn't miss what I couldn't see because, "faith is the things hoped for and the evidence of things not seen." (Hebrew 11:1) I wanted to make sure I was going in the right direction and doing all that God had planned for me in living out my faith. There are times in life where everything looks right, seems right, and you are even doing right, but you know there is something that just isn't right. So I decided to ask God to show me in his Word what more I was to do.

Living your best life is making sure that in living your best, you have exhausted all avenues of your purpose for being created in the first place. If I can go back to my dinner friend that I spoke of earlier, Dan, who retired as a physicist, he was not finished with all avenues of his purpose, and at sixty, went back to school, got another degree, and worked some more in a totally different field until he retired again.

So many people, young and old, have no idea about what they want to do, and they do not sense or understand their own self worth. Some young adults continue on through their twenties and thirties searching aimlessly to find themselves. So many older people retire, and after a few weeks, want to go back to their job because they feel useless not working for a living. What is most disturbing to me is that so many people lack a sense of purpose not realizing their value and worth as a human being. People often miss the value of simply sharing who they are and what the Lord has done for them with others.

For some of us, we openly admit that we do not know what to do with our lives. Some of us may know where to start and others at the end of their careers and don't have any idea of what to do next. There comes a time in everyone's life where they seek God for purpose and direction, even if they don't realize that is what they are seeking. This is why the scriptures tell us in Isaiah 55:6, "Seek the Lord while he may be found; call on Him while he is near..." There are times when we just

We all are connected, and need for those around us to be who God made them to be, and do what God has assigned them to do.

have to seek out God. This is important for all of us. We all are connected, and need for those around us to be who God made them to be, and do what God has assigned them to do. *"We are who we are because of who we all are."* It matters! Everybody can help somebody do something. The Bible puts it like this in Galatians 6:7, "Do not be deceived, God is not mocked: for whatever a man sows, that he will also reap." In short, if you help others, God will send others to help you.

Don't Settle, Live Out God's Promise For You

In searching for direction, we need to get our compass from God. The important lessons to remember here is don't settle. Let's dig a little deeper into the life of Abraham and Sarah. In Genesis 15, in verse one, God assured Abram that he would definitely have an heir. Straight from God himself, he tells Abraham in a vision, saying, "Do not be afraid, Abram, I am your shield, your exceedingly great reward." Abraham did what we all do at different times in our lives. Abraham could not see what God could do in his life from looking at his reality because in looking at his circumstances, it seemed hopeless. Abraham tries to tell God in verse two, "Lord God, what will you give me, seeing I go childless, and the heir of my house is Eliezer of Damascus? Look, you have given me no offspring; indeed, one born in my house is my heir!"

In other words, despite the fact that God himself promised Abraham that he would have an heir, he was willing to settle by having another man (Eliezer) in his household use his seed to bear Abraham an heir. This would have been kind of like adoption where Abraham figured he would just adopt Eliezer's son. Then God clarified it again for Abraham and God said to him in verses four and five, "This one shall not be your heir, but one who will come from your own body shall be your heir. Look now toward heaven, and count the stars if you are able to number them. So shall your descendants be." For the remainder of this chapter, God and Abraham communicated through Abraham's dreams. Abraham even offered a sacrifice up to God, and God continued to speak to Abraham.

Then, after all of that, Abraham still did not believe, and without a single word of objection, at the suggestion of his wife, Sarah, he took his wife's Egyptian maidservant, Hagar, and had relations with her as his wife. Abraham and Sarah settled instead of waiting and trusting God. Did God get angry and go back on his promise? No, God's plan for our lives doesn't change because we mess up. Remember, He is God, and He can still use us. Romans 8:28, tells us that all things work together for good to those who love the Lord, and to those who are called according to His purpose. Even though we make mistakes, the Word teaches us in First John 1:9 that, "If we confess our sins, He is faithful and just to forgive us and cleanse us from all unrighteousness."

After Abraham and Sarah went on many more journeys and life circumstances, according to God's appointed time, God brought into fruition what He had promised. Abraham was a century old, and Sarah was past childbearing years at the age of ninety. Before I go on, I just want to say, yes!!! Abraham and Sarah were rocking!!! According to Genesis 21:1-3, "And the Lord visited Sarah as He had said, and the Lord did for Sarah as He had spoken. For Sarah conceived and bore Abraham a son in his old age, at the set time of which God had spoken to him. And Abraham called the name of his son who was born to him, whom Sarah bore to him, Isaac."

How many times do we as believers take matters into our own hands, mess up things, and then, need God to come in and fix it? Unfortunately, sometimes when we take things into our own hands and settle instead of trusting God to carry out His purpose and plan, it has consequences that last for generations. Thus is the case with Abraham and Sarah. Here we are centuries later, watching the fierce battle of wills and disdain between the lineage of Ishmael and the lineage of Isaac, Abraham's two sons.

Nothing in the course of human history has happened outside of God's appointed time. If we trust God, there is nothing in our lives that He cannot turn around, work around or turn upside down for His glory and His purpose in His appointed time. The thing I love the most about God is that he keeps His Word in spite of us. When we are disobedient, God loves and restores us as we repent and seek Him. He doesn't cast us aside or dismiss us, but He keeps right on loving us and fulfilling His promises as we do His will.

The good news is that whether we are coming from a place of high esteem or low esteem, there is no partiality with God.

Consider this, it was never really about Abraham and Sarah in the first place. God wanted to create the lineage and bloodline for our Savior, Jesus Christ. Abraham and Sarah were the vessels He chose to use to carry out His plan in the appointed time. The good news is that whether we are coming from a place of high esteem or low esteem, there is no partiality with God. He wants us to choose not to settle. As we live our best life now, it is imperative that we get on board with a vengeance with what God is doing in, around and through us. God wants to work miracles in your life. We need to have a clear understanding how interwoven all of our lives are and that every single human life is of great value to God and should also be of great value to us. You are special to God.

PART II

GOD WANTS US TO HAVE A BLESSED LIFE

The thief does not come except to steal, and to kill, and to destroy. I have come that they might have life, and that they might have it more abundantly. *~John 10:10*

7 ~ YOU HAVE TO GUARD YOUR JOY

Have you ever met someone who seemed to have a perfect life? It seems they just have the best of luck in everything. Know anyone like that? Well, this section might not be for that lucky person who has managed to avoid the thief, but for the rest of us, let's talk about locking up the thief and guarding our joy to live victoriously. The Bible tells us in John 10:10, "The thief comes not, but for to steal, and to kill, and to destroy. I have come that they might have life, and have it more abundantly." The thief comes to steal every blessing that God has given us.

As we watch the world in turmoil, we see the enemy firsthand attacking mankind. The Bible teaches us that the thief comes to steal, kill, and destroy. But Jesus has promised to help us and bless us with an abundant life. In other words, Satan, the enemy of God, the thief, tries to mess up all that God created, but Jesus came to make sure the believer knows that He is able to ensure that we have an abundant and joyful life. In other words, like they used to say in my home church growing up, "Jesus is a mind regulator and heart fixer!"

The verse in John 10:10 was written as a warning to the believer and letting us know that God's enemy, the thief, would try his dead-level best to steal, kill and destroy us. Let's think about this because there is nothing worse than feeling defeated. Listen to what the first part of this verse says in John 10:10. It says the thief's only purpose is to hurt you. When you know that someone's sole purpose for existing is to destroy and harm you, your next step would be to gear up for battle or find a way to retreat. This is why we need to put on the full armor of God as outlined in Chapter 6 in the book of Ephesians. For some of us, the thief has almost killed us with struggles, trials and tribulations. We have had more than our share. Some of our struggles make us look back and know that it was only because of the sheer grace of God that kept us sound and in our right mind and still standing upright to talk about it. If you have endured struggles to that magnitude and have been victorious, take time to reflect and praise God you made it thus far, because many people did not make it at all.

Follow God's Direction

The thief wants to steal some key things from you that will rob you of your direction. It is so crucial to understand that the thief may try to steal in all areas of your life, but his number one motive is to keep you from God. The enemy does not want you to fulfill the purpose and plan that God has for your life. The enemy does not want you to understand your value and impact on those around you, and above all, he does not want you to value your relationship with God.

In the situation with Abraham and Sarah, the thief tried over and over to steal their faith, and they succumbed to it. The evidence is with the baby mama drama that Abraham had as a result of him not believing God and having a child with Hagar. The thief tries to steal our faith because it is the core of our relationship with God. Notice with Abraham and Sarah, throughout the course of their life, they struggled with disbelief as they continued to offer up sacrifices to God. Yet, God used them anyway. In the end, they were victorious because Satan is not God. He has no power over the will of almighty God, and Satan has no power over a human heart yielded to God. The Word lets us know in Romans 8:37 that, "We are more than conquerors through Him who loved us." Like all of us, Abraham and Sarah were human, and though they made mistakes as all humans do, they continued to believe in God resulting in a great impact on mankind.

As believers, we need to embrace our humanness. God could have opted to make us more robotic. He didn't because He wanted us to love Him freely, and have faith in Him with our own free will. When we do, God pours out so much mercy and grace in our lives. In Psalms 100:5, the psalmist puts it this way, "For the Lord is good; His mercy is everlasting, and His truth endures to all generations." Abraham, the father of the Israelites, and Sarah, the mother of the Israelites, who started the lineage of our Savior, showed a lack of faith over and over, and yet God never stopped loving them or using them. They had a relationship with Him, and they kept working at following God's directions.

As a result of Abraham and Sarah's relationship with the Lord, He had a hedge of protection around them. He watched over them. Even, as we read in Genesis, when Abraham kept lying to save his own life in telling different kings that Sarah was his sister so they wouldn't kill him for her, God intervened and made sure no harm came to either one of them. All through their lives, they continued to doubt God right up to the time Sarah's ninety-year-old body and Abraham's one-hundred-year old body witnessed the birth of the heir that God promised them. They didn't understand that God wanted to work a miracle through them and that it was all about His timing and not theirs.

God understands our humanness and will work out the plan and purpose that He has for us. I love this story of Abraham and Sarah because it epitomizes The Jael Effect of how God can use us through all our mess

I love this story of Abraham and Sarah because it epitomizes The Jael Effect of how God can use us through all our mess ups.

ups. If we will move out of the way, God will work out His plan for our lives. God understands our lack of faith, and He promises that if we have just a tiny bit of faith, He will do a phenomenal work in our lives. Jesus said in Matthew 17:20, "Because of your unbelief, for assuredly, I say to you, if you have faith as a mustard seed, you will say to this mountain, 'Move from here to there,' and it will move; and nothing will be impossible to you." Pray and ask God to help your unbelief and allow Him to use you anyway.

Moving Past Your Own Understanding

John 10:10 also teaches us that the thief wants to kill us. Oftentimes, when we read this passage, we think about how the enemy may try to end our life through sickness, disease, violence and self-destruction. This and more is the truth. Let's be real. The world is full of death, and God has allowed it to be so. Years ago, while working as a teacher at a high school, I had a beautiful young lady in my class we will call Jennifer. She was an outgoing young lady, who was tall, had beautiful skin, long black hair and simply gorgeous. However, she was a little edgy, and I had really been working with her to build a good relationship and help her be successful in my class. Trust developed between us, and she shared with me that she wanted to be a model. One Friday, before we left for the weekend, I talked to Jennifer about the goals she had for her life. I was feeling good because I had been successful in developing a rapport with her, and she had shown improvement overall.

Over the weekend, Jennifer was in the car with some friends, and as they were going through an intersection, another driver ran a stop sign hitting Jennifer's side of the car. The impact of the accident killed her immediately making her the only fatality in the car. What a lot of people do not know about educators is that most of us care about our students so deeply that they literally become our day children. Not only was Jennifer's family devastated, we at the school, teachers, administrators, and students alike, grieved immensely. We as believers just have to know that God also grieves when we go through life's tragedies. Death is real, but if you are reading this book, then, it is because God has allowed you to live for yet another day. If you have no other reason to praise Him, you can praise Him for yet another moment of life, another thought, another breath. Sometimes we just need to have faith beyond our own understanding and trust God.

Trust God's Word

Let me pause for a moment here because before I became a believer, I really struggled with how good people had to endure so much pain. Even as a believer these last few decades, I have had to continually go back to the Word for answers. As a Creationist, I believe our story begins in Genesis Chapter one. It is important to understand that when God originally created humans, He created us and placed us in the Garden of Eden, a perfect environment. Genesis 2:15 says, "Then, the Lord God took the man and put him in the Garden of Eden to tend and keep it." Death did not exist in God's original plan, Eden was paradise, but God warned Adam in verse 16-17 of the same chapter, "And the Lord God commanded the man, saying, "Of every tree of the garden you may freely eat; but of the tree of the knowledge of good and evil, you shall not eat, for in the day that you eat of it, you shall surely die." When Adam disobeyed God, death now entered into humanity. The enemy wants to destroy mankind with death. In Job 1:7, God helps us to see this through a conversation He has with Satan asking, "From where do you come?" Satan answered, "From going to and fro on the earth, and from walking back and forth on it."

Since Eden, the enemy has been having a field day with man. However, God gave us a freewill, and we have the power to make choices in dealing with the world around us. This is why God tells us in James 4:7, "Therefore submit to God. Resist the devil, and he will flee from you." The other point to note is that God intervenes in the affairs of man. A hard reality is that God wants us to choose to serve Him and not his enemy. He allows the enemy to torment and tempt us. Consider what happened to Job. The enemy wanted to kill and utterly destroy Job's life, but God only allowed him to go so far. The overall lesson learned from this story is that nothing on this Earth happens unless God allows it to be so. God has a purpose and a plan for everyone's life, and He is not finished with us. To put it simply, if God was finished with us, we would be dead. Think about Jael with me for a moment. Jael just did what needed to be done to save the nation that would give birth our Lord and Savior, Jesus Christ.

While Satan may want us dead, he can only do what God allows. In the story, God boasted to Satan about Job being upright and choosing Him. Satan says to God in Job 1:9-11, "Does Job fear God for nothing? Have you not made a hedge around him, around his household and around all that he has on every side? You have blessed the work of his hands, and his possessions have increased in the land. But now, stretch out your hand and touch all that he has, and he will surely curse you to your face!" Nothing happens to us outside of God's plan. He strategically has placed us. That is why we hear about incredible life saving miracles and walk away baffled. There are times in my life that I knew the only reason I survived, stayed in my right mind, made it through, and lived is because God had a hedge around me and blessed me. I am praying right now that someone is reading this and understands what this verse teaches us. You cannot miss this because God needs us to share this message.

The message is this, that no matter what we have been doing, or what we have been through or what we will go through, God has a purpose, a plan, and a work that He wants to carry out with the life that He gave us. God can work around us! That includes our failures, sadness, family, friends, career and even our successes! Furthermore, it is important to understand that from the beginning to the end of Job's life, God used Job for His purpose and His glory.

As believers, God wants us to trust Him and to love him unconditionally. This is all about our relationship with Christ and allowing Him to use us to carry out the purpose He has for us!!! God allowed His enemy to harm Job to prove a point and teach a lesson to us. Look at what the Lord said to Satan in Job 1:12, "Behold, all that he has in your power; only do not lay a hand on his person." God was in control. God allowed Satan to harm Job, but made it very clear not to kill him. Thus, Satan caused havoc in Job's life destroying everything he had, everyone he loved and inflicted Job with severe boils all over his body. Job had no help from his friends. Instead of comforting Job, they started telling him that he must have sinned. Job had no help from his wife. Job's wife told him that he should just curse God and die. As for Job's children, God allowed Satan to kill them.

Job was left to just look to the God he loved; the God who had blessed him and watched over him all those years. Without being able to make sense of any of the horrific things happening to him, Job argued with God, not understanding any of it. God talked with Job. In His conversation with Job, God was clear in declaring His authority as the God of all creation to do whatever He pleased. All along the underlying question was whether or not God would allow the enemy to break Job so he would curse God and die. However, the scriptures tell us in 1 Corinthians 10:13 (NIV) that, "No temptation has overtaken you except what is common to mankind. And God is faithful; He will not let you be tempted beyond what you can bear. But when you are tempted, He will also provide a way out so that you can endure it."

Believe In God's Plan

Because of Job's story, we have a story. As with Job, in our relationship with God, He places a hedge around our lives. In understanding Job's story, we see God's sovereignty. This teaches us that whatever happens in our lives, God can use us. Notice, Job's story is in the Bible. Job was an ordinary rich man just living his life. Perhaps the the lesson for us to learn is that whether it is through foreseen or unforeseen circumstances, or through self-inflicted choices, God can work in, outside, under, over, around, and through us to carry out His purpose and His plan for our lives. But, the question is, will we love and trust Him? Will we have that mustard seed of faith to know in our hearts that God is doing a work in our lives? Job's story is for us. In all that he lost and suffered through, look at what it says in Job 1:20-22, "Then Job arose, tore his robe, and shaved his head; and he fell to the ground and worshiped. And he said: "Naked I came from my mother's womb and naked shall I return there. The Lord gave, and the Lord has taken away. Blessed be the name of the Lord. In all this, Job did not sin nor charge God with wrong."

Once we understand that God has a hedge around us and blesses us, then, we can understand how He is not going to let anything happen to us outside of His purpose. In other words, whatever has happened to you, you can still carry out God's purpose. While the enemy has not taken your life, it is only because God has not allowed him to. Therefore, what the enemy will do, since he can't take your life, he will try to kill other things in your life. There needs to be a sense of urgency in carrying out our God-given assignments. To do that, we have to be cognizant that God's enemy is also our enemy and our opposition, and he wants to kill everything in us.

God's enemy will start with our relationships. The thief attempts to sabotage our lives through our relationships. As we move forward in our lives, it is time to get our relationships right. Do not dwell on failed marriages or failed relationships in the past. If there is a need to restore, make up or apologize to someone, let this be a priority. In Romans 12:18, the Bible teaches that, "If it is possible, as much as depends on you, live peacefully with all men (mankind)." As believers, we are ambassadors of God's kindness and grace. No matter how hard it gets, we have to continue to strive to show the world the love of Christ through our relationships. Remember my adaptation of Ubuntu? *"We are who we are because of who we all are."* We need each other. We all matter. Your wholeness encompasses the wholeness of others.

Consider 1st John 4:20, "If someone says, 'I love God, and hates his brother, he is a liar; for he who does not love his brother whom he has seen, how can he love God whom he has not seen?" We are flawed in our humanness, and there are times when we may have problems with people. The enemy will make sure of that. He wants to destroy every relationship we have in our lives. This includes relationships with our family and friends, relationships with people of other races and even relationships with our own selves. Yet, God continues in the same chapter in 1st John in verse 21, "And this commandment we have from Him, that he who loves God must love his brother also."

Let's back up for a moment, because one of the things that seems to be missing as we witness people making mistakes that have detrimental national and international impact is the lack of repentance. As we read in the very first book in the Bible, we know God's enemy and all his demons are out to destroy God's beautiful creation. The Bible reveals this evil. For many of us, as we witness the atrocities that human beings are committing against other human beings, what is shocking is the arrogance, the boldness, and the in-your-face hatred of people who simply are not remorseful and outright evil in their dealings. There seems to be no regard for other lives created and ordained by God as established in Genesis; lives created in the image and in the likeness of God.

We have all failed at one point or another. We have to embrace our mistakes. There is good news. First John 1:9, "If we confess our sins, God is faithful and just to forgive us our sins and to cleanse us from all unrighteousness." Even though we may have messed up in our behavior and in our relationships, God still can use us and work around our flaws. However, as children of God, we are to be of good moral character. We do need to make sure things are right with the people God has placed in our lives. However, after we have done all we can to get things right, we have to leave the outcome in God's hands. Once we repent by asking God for forgiveness, and once we ask forgiveness of those we have offended, we are free. Our miracles have to include us embracing God's forgiveness and grace. We must also embrace our own flaws and forgive ourselves understanding that to extend grace to ourselves is to extend it to others because we are all flawed and need forgiveness and grace.

This is the first step to freedom of guilt and shame. However, there are times when our mistakes are so grave and hurtful to others that it requires more than just an apology. As we will examine, a prime example of this is the life of the Apostle Paul. Our mistakes may require that we use the same rigor we used when we messed up to fix all that that we did to harm and hurt other people. True repentance requires action. There are times when our mess ups give purpose to our lives because it requires our lives turning around to fix all that we have done or to fix that which we have broken. This is the essence of The Jael Effect in turning our mistakes into miracles of change; into miracles of good and all that is decent in the eyes of God, demonstrating love for all that He created and deemed as very good.

8 ~ START FROM WHERE YOU ARE

In the last chapter, we looked at how the enemy tries to steal, kill and destroy us, but the story does not stop there, in John 10:10, the verse continues, "...but I have come that you might have life and have it more abundantly." In the early twentieth century, addressing what the Black community needed to do to move forward, Booker T. Washington made a profound statement that I continue to carry with me, "Lay down your buckets from where you are." In other words, as it comes to living life abundantly, wherever you are, decide to start right there to experience life abundantly within your circumstances. This is important because the battle of life is between your two ears, the mind. If you can start praising God while living in hell, you have already won because you have found the secret of full joy in Christ. Understanding that He is all powerful and can work miracles in His time in your circumstances according to His will.

If you can start praising God while living in hell, you have already won because you have found the secret of full joy in Christ.

Think about these nine profound words of Jesus and what He is saying to us, "But I have come that you might have life...." In John 1:3, the Word tells us that all things were made through Jesus, and without Jesus, nothing was made. As our creator, Jesus came to earth and interacted with humans as a man to endure the punishment for our imperfections and sins against God. Our redemption in Christ allows us to have an abundant and fulfilled life.

In Ecclesiastes 9:10 NLT, it teaches that, "Whatever you do, do well. For when you go to the grave, there will be no work or planning or knowledge or wisdom." We need to embrace our roles in the world and understand that we are the champions, and God wants us to live as champions and live victoriously!

So often, we live our lives forgetting that we are on the clock. It is important to remember that there is no waiting. For every breath you breathe, for every time your heart beats, that is a moment in your life that you will not get back. In other words, if you are a single person waiting for a mate, live your best life in your singlehood because the work that God has for you right now, He wants to do it with you as a single person.

If you are a married person, waiting for your spouse to disappear, understand that God knows what you are going through, and there are times when we need to pick up our cross and walk the path God has laid out for us. If you are within God's will, He has a work equipped for you within your marriage. I want you to notice that, after Jesus warned us what the thief was going to do in the first part of the verse, he then used the conjunction word 'but'. The word 'but' means to introduce something contrasting with what has already been mentioned. In short, Jesus used 'but' to tell us that defeat does not have to be our story because He came to make sure that we live victoriously, whether single or married!

Being in the center of God's will is to have an abundant life. After Jesus said he wants us to have life, he used the conjunction word 'and,' which is used to connect words and sentences together with each other. It doesn't matter who you are or where you live in the world. If you are not in the center of God's will for your life, you will feel that something is missing because you are not living the purpose and plan of why God created you.

I noticed that in writing and sharing with you, I felt free. I knew that for me, this was about fulfilling a purpose that God had for my life. I told you early on that we were in this together. That we are going through a journey together in answering the question of how we can be more, do more and be used to the fullest extent by Jesus. We need to reject the

Live your most abundant life with a vengeance, on purpose, now!

world's standard of who gets to be rated as beautiful or smart or victorious or even successful. This is your life! We all get to be our own beautiful, our own smart and our own victorious. We need to embrace who we are as conquerors and survivors, and praise God for giving us another day. Live your most abundant life with a vengeance, on purpose, now!

Like My Grandmother

My paternal grandmother, Mamie, was a great example of living your best life, and also, I might add, another Jael. She and grandpa gave us a huge family. Before having their family, she and my grandfather married and moved from South Carolina to Steelton, Pennsylvania. They opened a small community corner store and raised ten children in the apartment on top of the store. My grandfather passed away when I was in elementary school, but he lived to see his children grow up and have families.

My father loved his parents. After we moved from Harrisburg, Pennsylvania, my father would load us in the car to visit them several times a year. This continued even after my grandfather passed. Incidentally, Harrisburg is the capital of Pennsylvania outside of Steelton, and also the home of Three Mile Island. Even Harrisburg has a story to tell. My grandmother had a daughter, my Aunt Gertrude, who lived at home until she married in her thirties. After Aunt Gertrude got married and moved out of the house, my grandmother wasn't ready to retire from doing the one thing she loved, which was to raise children. Therefore, she once again filled the small apartment on top of the store with children. My grandmother fostered three sisters until they were grown, and they were older children, not babies. I had three new aunts my age and a little older.

For my grandmother, this was living out her purpose and plan that God had for her, and in that season of her life, she gave unconditional love and saved three people from entering adulthood without a family. She passed away with a sense of fulfillment and with a community of people around her saying nice things about how her life touched theirs.

Some would say that living abundantly is about collecting material possessions. But let's imagine this, in one room of the funeral home was my grandmother, whose family disowned her for marrying outside of her social class, but who blessed so many lives being a pastor's wife, a community store owner and a mother. Imagine in another room, laid a local millionaire woman who had just a couple of children who came to pay their respects, but never got to know their mother because she was about making money and living for herself. The millionaire passed away with prestige but sad and alone in a huge empty house.

My grandmother passed away with a small apartment on top of her little community store filled with love in the arms of her family who absolutely adored her. My grandmother epitomized how living an abundant life is not about how much you have but about how much you love and live in the center of God's will in carrying out the purpose and plan that he has for your life in each season.

Like the Apostle Paul

Saul, whom God renamed to Paul after his conversion, was a well-educated man of his day. I suppose Paul was also considered wealthy as a Roman General, but one thing is for sure, he was a powerful Jael spirit and a force to be reckoned with. He was considered of high esteem and respected by his peers. Yet, he lacked compassion and character, and many poor Christians suffered horrible deaths at the command of Saul. Saul approved of the stoning of Stephen, a beloved Christian leader as recorded in the Book of Acts 7:58. Yet, God in all His mercy and in accordance to His divine plan called out Saul on that Damascus Road. The change and the light that Paul would illuminate for the cause of Christ had to be reflected in even the changing of his name because he was deeply feared by everyone that knew him. This is why prior to the Damascus experience; this oppressive Roman General was renamed Paul. After his conversion, with his knowledge of philosophy and religion under his new name, Paul could debate with the most educated scholars of his day.

A miracle happened on that Damascus road. We see in the Book of Acts how the position and status of a man that had done pure evil was turned around to be used for good. Instead of persecuting killing Christians, Paul helped and served the very people and God he hated. Additionally, God also used Paul's training and intellectual capability to write thirteen books in the New Testament.

As a high official in the Roman Empire, Saul built his prestige on the torment of Christians in the early church. Acts 9:1-19; 22:6-21; 26:12-18. While the Bible tells the story of how God reached out to Paul on the Damascus Road, the most important story is that God had mercy and forgave Paul for all his mistakes in killing all those Christians. On the road to Damascus, God blinded Paul. Then, God told one of his disciples, Ananias, to go and heal Paul's eyes and baptize him. Ananias expressed his concern to God because, after all, Paul tortured and killed Christians. Listen to the words of Jesus to Ananias regarding Paul in Acts 9:15-16, "Go, for he is a chosen vessel of Mine to bear My name before Gentiles, kings, and the children of Israel. For I will show him how many things he must suffer for My name's sake." God called Paul to use as His vessel for His purpose according to His plan in His time.

He called him out right in the midst of his sins. Later, as Paul went on his journey in preaching for the Lord and sharing his testimony, he shared with people in Acts: 22:10, that he had to ask the Lord what he should do and that the Lord told him to go to Damascus and wait for instructions.

God can and does use any of us at any time according to His purpose. Perhaps from Paul's story, we can see that after we have lived doing whatever we have been doing, God is still calling us out for a purpose. It is important that we do not miss this. Let's read as Paul reveals his conversation with God in Acts 26:15-12, "So I said, 'Who are You, Lord?' And He said, 'I am Jesus, whom you are persecuting. But rise and stand on your feet: for I have appeared to you for this purpose, to make you a minister and a witness both of the things which you have seen and of the things which I will yet reveal to you…"

Whenever God calls us to do something, it will require a response of submission.

God called out Saul and changed his name to Paul. He called Paul out, and then used Paul's testimony to show the early church then, and us today, that He is all-powerful, and as He did then and will do now. God will call us out to use us for His purpose and His plan. However, whenever God calls us to do something, it will always require a response of submission.

100

We have to say yes to Him. God wants people who will willingly love and serve Him. To live abundantly and have the fullness of joy, we need to fully submit to allowing God to use us and live in the center of His will for our lives. Despite all of his mistakes, God called out Paul for a divine assignment. However, Paul had to surrender his will to God so that the power of the Holy Spirit could manifest through him to reach multitudes changing countless lives.

9 ~ TELL YOUR STORY

When you look at the life of Paul, you may wonder why God did not call Paul out earlier in his life before he tormented, persecuted, and murdered so many Christians. Just think about all the lives that would have been spared. But in looking at his life a little closer, there is a truth here that cannot be missed. God is always in control, and His purpose for our lives is in conjunction with His plan. In answering the prayers of the Israelites, we can look back at Jael's story and see how God had her in place at the right time to slay Sisera, the army commander at war with the Israelites. The Israelites cried out asking God to help them, and He answered.

Everything is about God's timing, not ours. While God does not condone or endorse our sins, it is through the blood of Jesus that we are sanctified and cleansed. Paul is the epitome of God's grace and how He alone can work miracles in our lives to carry out His divine will. Paul thought that he was in control and was full of himself, but in God's appointed time, He blinded and called Paul out on the Damascus Road. Isn't it interesting how Paul, the one killing and persecuting all the Jesus followers, knew immediately who Jesus was? Paul immediately yielded to God's purpose and plan for his life. Paul made the decision to follow God and found his true purpose in life. Wherever we are in our relationship with God, when God calls us out, we would be wise to answer. Psalms 111:10, puts it this way, "The fear of the Lord is the beginning of wisdom; A good understanding have all those who do His commandments. His praise endures forever." This reminds of a play I went to see years ago called, 'Your Arms Are Too Short To Box With God."

Using Your Life Experiences

That is why we need to understand the significance of who we are because God watches over us throughout our entire lives, and regardless of what we are doing, God knows we belong to Him. What God has for us is intentional. God has a purpose for our existence and wants to use us from the beginning to end. Watch the truth connoted in Jeremiah 29:11, *"For I know the plans I have for you," declares the Lord, "plans to prosper you and not to harm you, plans to give you hope and a future."* God wants to see us prosper in all things, and in Psalms 91:11, it lets us know that He has given His angels charge over us to keep us in all of our ways as we serve out His plans for us. God placed you where you are for His divine purpose!

A few years ago, I led a mission's trip to Kenya, and our mission's team of twenty-two met with a Kenyan evangelical team once we got there. We were ministering with them in various locations and villages. These Kenyans were on fire for the Lord, and in one of our group sessions, I remember asking them about their needs. One of the things they told us was that they needed more Christian resources and literature because the people wanted to grow as believers but lacked resources. As an American with so many Christian resources everywhere, it was hard to believe that was even an issue, but it was indeed. Hearing this reminded me that I had heard the same thing from a Christian man that I met walking through the streets in Khartoum, Sudan, in East Africa. He told me that new Sudanese converts often struggled because they lacked Christian resources to grow as believers. Sudan is a strict Muslim country and Christians there have had a history of severe persecution, especially in the South.

I found this to be the case again when taking a team to Honduras with my organization Educators International Service, Inc. (EIS). In the summer of 2014, we partnered with Adventures in Christ Ministry and went to Honduras. EIS educators provided professional development at the invitation of some of the schools there and donated and distributed educational supplies. In asking one of the Christian school directors what was needed at the school, she expressed the need to have Bibles to give out to the children, and laptops to train them how to use the computer. One school had a room with the drops set up for computers all ready. They were just praying for the furniture and computers to finish outfitting the room for a computer class.

These examples will help us to see Jeremiah 29:11 in a different context. Whether in Kenya, Sudan or Honduras, living abundantly in Christ is about living in the fullness of joy and being in the center of God's will allowing Him to work out His purpose and His plan for our life regardless of where we live. In the case of my Hondurans, Sudanese and Kenyan friends, the one thing they all had in common was their passion for the work they were doing in their service to God and the people. Regardless of our location, God placed us there, and He needs for all of us to carry out our assignment using our experiences for His glory.

One of the most profound tactics of the enemy is to work on our inner thoughts. The enemy, whether in the spiritual world or physical world, tries to distort who we think we are and what we think we can accomplish. The people we think are the strongest often fall right before our eyes, and those we think are weak, we see rising up. My mother often quotes James 4:6, "God resists the proud, but gives grace to the humble." The best defense, whatever your position, is to stand on the Word of God. In Romans 8:37, it tells us, "Yet in all these things, we are more than conquerors through him who loved us." This is why it is important to know your worth according to who the Bible says you are and to go forth with confidence in moving forward with what God has called you to do.

Some companies only require that you account for the last five to ten years on your resume. Many of us have worked at several different companies or organizations throughout our lives. It is important to understand that God's purpose and plan encompassed everything and every place we ever worked. In fact, God's purpose and plan embodies everything you have ever been, everyone you have ever met and all that you have ever experienced. All of that and more have brought you to this point in your life to be used by God, whether young or old, rich or poor, black, white, brown or yellow, which leads to a very important credential that you have, your experience.

In 1 Peter 1:20, it tells us that God's plan and purpose for us was preordained before the foundations of the world. For those of us who have children, we have good and bad experiences as being parents. To be honest, some of us need to repent and start being better parents immediately. Some of us were simply not good parents, and now, our children are grown. But with Christ, there is always redemption. We can make up for it with our grandchildren and other children in our lives. Maybe we can be a blessing to other mothers and fathers by encouraging and helping them.

Let's look at this another way, we all may have some experience in working with people at different times and in different venues, such as with our family, school, store, bank, church, recreation, work, even in applying for work. While the value of these experiences may be underestimated, all of these are lessons that we learned and skills that we acquired. Whatever lessons we learn or skills that we acquire, we can share with someone, especially someone younger than us.

In our relationships, we have learned by multiple experiences how to be successful with difficult or challenging people and have lived through difficult situations. We have learned lessons in our romantic relationships that can be useful in encouraging someone. As believers, all of us are called in Matthew 5:16 to be a light for God to model and teach others to respect and love one another. We are also called to teach the truth about humanity in Genesis 1:26, Psalms 8: 4-9, Psalms 139:14, John 3:16, Romans 2:11 and Acts 10:34-35. Additionally, all believers are to model how we are to value all human life and appreciate the sanctity and beauty of all that God created. Please take time to meditate with me on these scriptures above so we can walk in unison and be right with God.

In working in the school system, I see young people everyday in need of mentors in their environment to teach them how to be successful in building a rapport with people. Skills we may take for granted, like how to speak to adults, especially ones in authority, or how to look someone in the eye when speaking with them, or how to greet another person. These are skills children need to learn at home from their parents, grandparents, aunts and uncles, but unfortunately, this is not always the case. It leaves a great void in our society when we don't reach back and grab hold to someone coming up behind us. This is at any age.

Most people have someone younger who is looking up to them. It may even be people we don't know. It is up to us to determine how we use our life experiences to influence and impact others. The lessons that you have learned are invaluable. Teach them either from your successes or teach them from your failures. Even if you did not get it right, it is not too late to teach and help others to do it right. Sometimes the best teachers were the learners who struggled the most. Simply be your authentic self and walk in the integrity of God's grace, love and mercy.

Turning A Painful Past Into a Joyful Future

Many of us have struggled throughout our lives and may feel broken, wore out and even defeated. Some of us look beautiful from the outside—beautiful bodies, homes, families, careers and friends—but internally, our hearts are filled with pain. Behind the beautiful façade, there may be emptiness, depression, emotional or physical abuse, neglect and hurt. In God's providence, all that happened to us was within His control, and He wants to use our experiences for His glory.

Consider this, John 9:1-5 tells the story of a man who suffered from blindness. The disciples asked Jesus, "Who sinned, the blind man, or his parents, that he should be blind?" Jesus' answer reveals a deep truth that helps us to understand that we all must live our lives right where God has placed us because it is in that position that God wants to do His work through us. Every one, every place, every day is involved indirectly or directly in the plan of God. Jesus said to His disciples, *"Neither did this man sin, nor his parents: but that the works of God should be made manifest in him."* I know many people may not want to hear this, but this scripture is teaching us that this is not heaven, and we are going to have some trials and tribulations. But Jesus said, regardless of your circumstance or situation, God wants to reveal His glory through our circumstances and experiences.

If you can be thankful for your life in whatever circumstances you have had to endure, then, you have the victory and have defeated the enemy. When you can be grateful to God and have faith in the midst of your pain and suffering, you have just discovered what it really means to live life more abundantly and to have real joy. One of the highest platforms of Christian growth is the understanding of God's total sovereignty over the affairs of men, and that He not only has all power and all control, but He has and will reign forever. Perhaps if the blind man hadn't been blind, he would have never come to know Christ, and in considering this even further, perhaps if the blind man hadn't suffered from blindness, all of the people who witnessed this miracle of his sight being restored would have never believed.

In sharing from my own life, one of the beautiful things about living in Orlando was that my friends and family would often come to visit while vacationing. Some even had a second home there. One of my girlfriends came to town, and we were on our way somewhere when I shared this personal story with her. I am not quite sure how it happened, but I ended up sharing some deeply personal stories from my childhood. With tears in her eyes, she urged me to share my story with others because she said it would help so many people. I told her that I didn't see the point because I have dealt with it, moved on, and never wanted to be defined or feel defeated from my troubles. But for some reason, her words have stayed with me, and since I have been on this close journey with you, perhaps it will help you, or someone you know, in some way. That is a biblical principle taught in Second Corinthians 1:3-4, "Praise be to the God and Father of our Lord Jesus Christ, the Father of compassion and the God of all comfort, who comforts us in all troubles, so that we can comfort those in any trouble with the comfort we ourselves received from God."

As a young girl, I was molested. This seems quite ironic being the daughter of such Godly people serving in ministry, but even the best of parents can't always protect their children, especially since some of the very people they trusted were the ones hurting me. I don't know why God allowed it to happen, but I know as a result of it, I have such a deep compassion for people who are disadvantaged, hurting, and struggling, women and young people in particular. God has used this in my life to advocate for children and give me empathy in my work as an educator, on the mission field, and in ministry helping people from all ages and backgrounds.

I never had the deserved innocence of a child who didn't know about sex because when I was a little girl, the teenage sons of a babysitter used to try to teach me and their little brother, who was my age, how to have sex with each other for their own amusement. That was my initial introduction to the birds and the bees. Of course, we were so confused and ashamed we couldn't actually do anything, but what a way to learn about sex. Some of the people, who should have been protecting me, mistreated me. These times were the pre-Oprah days, and no one ever talked about such things. I must have learned that as a child because I didn't know what to do, and like most children, I internalized it and was silenced with shame until I became an adult.

God's Healing

We need to share our stories for the good of others who may need healing or who may need to know that our struggles do not need to define who we are. God can provide both healing and grace. Don't let the enemy use your sorrow, pain, abuse, sins and mistakes to define you. When you have dramatic experiences in your life, the pain will manifest itself in different ways. An example would be that pain manifests itself as a teenager having a really low self-image. But that same teen, can decide to use that pain and turn it around by becoming a teen that reaches out and befriends unpopular kids. Being someone who may have been taken advantage of can give you empathy for others who are picked on and even help you to advocate for them as well as yourself. Pain can also teach you to be strong and self-sufficient, which will equip you for the assignment and tasks that God has for you.

We all have things in our past that bring us great pain. No one leaves this earth unscathed. Some may hurt more so than others, but God sees it all. Somehow God allowed this evil to enter my life as a girl growing up, and it stole my innocence. By the sheer grace of God and because I had a wonderful mother and father who loved me, I wanted to rise above it, and I would read self-help psychology books as a teen. I also kept journals and worked through it. I also worked with inner city teens and became a counselor and literally healed myself by trying to heal everybody else. I believe that if you heal others, you heal yourself, and that if you help others, you help yourself. When I shared my story with my friend, I told her I shared it a few times with people I knew, but I just never wanted this to define who I am. This is one of few times I have shared it because I understand that with every experience, good or bad, it makes us who we are, and God can use it for His glory.

"We are who we are because of who we all are." Our lives are interconnected. We all have the right to just be and serve God within our experiences and circumstances. God is no respecter of persons. God can heal, fix, deliver, and use anybody at any time in any way He deems for His purpose and His glory. When I learned how to praise and worship, I could feel myself being healed deep within my soul. I was giving praise and adoration to God, and He was giving me joy, healing, peace, and deliverance. If you are a believer reading

this book, and you do not know what I am talking about, I am here as a witness that God can work a miracle deep within your inner self and heal you, deliver you and give you peace to be comfortable and feel loved in your own skin. Praise and worship through whatever circumstances you are going through and what will result from it is true joy. This is because your joy will then not be a result of your circumstances, but rather a result of your surrender and faith in God. You can never out bless God. If you praise Him in adoration, it is a reciprocal interaction, while you are praising and pouring out to Him, God is healing and pouring joy and peace into you.

We need to understand that we are on a divine assignment from the Creator himself, and our lives are intertwined with others for this purpose and time in human history. We all need each other. As believers, we must be very careful not to allow others to define who we are. Fight the urge! The center of our belief about ourselves and others needs to be grounded in who God says we are, and this is clear in Hebrews 2:7, which says that "we are a little lower than the angels." We are covered through the blood of Christ, and we are children of God. We need to simply live for Him because to do that is to realize that we have been placed on Earth in a time, space and place on purpose for Him. In all of our personal journeys, time is of essence. No single event defines our personhood. God is the author and finisher of our faith and who we are in Christ Jesus!

Using Your Talents Like Grandma Moses

There may be untapped talents and resources within you that God wants to use. It is crucial that we understand that wherever you are and whatever your circumstances, God needs you to surrender to His purpose for your life right within your space because His love is for every human being, and He needs people in every part of the globe to reach people in every part of the globe. This means in the hospital, prison and some of the most far-reaching places on earth. There is no space on earth where God will not shine His mercy and love. What is important is that we surrender in accordance with His timing.

Living through the World Pandemic COVID-19 has taught us that circumstances can change quickly and that you just can't assume that you will be able to do something at a certain age or at a certain time. We simply have to trust God's timing, even if we don't always understand. We need to carry out our God-given assignment and use our talents in His timing, young or old, regardless of age.

A perfect example of understanding God's timing in using the talents and gifts that we have is Anna Mary Robertson Moses, or as she was affectionately called,

Grandma Moses, another Jael who used what was in her hands. She lived from September 7, 1860, to December 13, 1961. I first learned about Grandma Moses years ago. She was an American folk artist who became famous creating beautiful paintings of her experiences in living in rural America. Grandma Moses' story is an example of why we need to use the talents and gifts within us, even the ones we have not tapped into yet.

Grandma Moses grew up in New York on a farm, and her daddy used to love to see his children draw so he would buy blank newspapers for them to draw pictures. Grandma Moses seemed to have a rather happy family life, and at age twelve, she began working as a live-in housekeeper and did so for fifteen years. During this time, she married a farm boy in her community. One of the families she worked for noticed her love for prints and gave her art materials for drawings. However, for the next few decades, Grandma Moses stayed busy as a wife, mother, and a farm worker. In fact, she gave birth to ten children but only five survived their infancy. Eventually, Grandma Moses and her husband bought their own farm. Interested in art, she embroidered beautiful pieces she made from yarn until her arthritis became unbearable in her seventies.

Now, here is what I want you to notice, Grandma Moses was in her seventies when she gave up embroidery due to arthritis, but it is important to notice how her life's work was not done. In fact, at the urging of her sister, she would start in her mid seventies the work that would make her famous. Grandma Moses probably never even imagined the attention her paintings would get and how people from all over the world would come to appreciate her work. From her arthritic hand she started painting and took the world by storm, becoming one of the most renowned American folk artists of her time painting the beautiful scenes and people from the farm life that she loved. Grandma Moses epitomizes how a person can successfully start an assignment or bless humanity at any age.

Don't allow negative thinking or negative people to have power in your life. To live an abundant and joyful life, it is crucial to reject negativity. Surround yourself with positive people. Grandma Moses' works have been shown and sold in the United States and abroad and have been marketed on greeting cards and other merchandise. Grandma Moses' paintings are among the collections of many museums. The *Sugaring Off* was sold for US $1.2 million in 2006. She wrote an

We each are a part of God's puzzle, and every piece is needed for completion.

autobiography, appeared on magazine covers, television and won numerous awards and two honorary doctoral degrees. Grandma Moses even has a documentary out about her life. It is never too late or too early to use the gifts and talents that God has given you to use here on this Earth. We all need what God has given each of us to share to bless each other. This is because, "we are who we are because of who we all are." We each are part of God's puzzle, and every piece is needed for completion.

10 ~ ABOUT YOUR LIFE'S LESSONS .

As we move forward, we need to look beyond our schooling and careers and what we have done in the past, but rather search deep and look beyond the obvious within ourselves. This may sound strange, but is necessary to find that which may be hidden within us. We need to look at our talents that may have been put on the back burner and can be reignited like Grandma Moses. Notice that the artwork was not far from the reality in which she lived. Her paintings were reflective of the life she lived in rural America. She painted about the people, places and experiences she encountered. As I have embarked on this journey, I have realized that is exactly what I am doing now. I am writing about the people, places and experiences I have encountered and the knowledge that I have learned.

Your Impact is Happening Now

As an educator and daughter of the church, I used every talent that was in me. I used leadership, public speaking, counseling, teaching, creativity, planning, singing, piano playing, and nurturing skills. In starting churches, I served as the business manager negotiating deals on buildings and such. When married, I served in the churches in Mississippi, Maryland, New York, and Florida. In these churches, I worked

119

closely the renovations for the buildings that needed to be fixed up. The same was true with leading a building project in The Gambia, West Africa, and with leading a building project with a middle school in Orlando, Florida. Serving in churches, I was the church pianist, main soloist and praise team leader. Over the years, between being a pastor's daughter and a pastor's wife in small churches where we didn't have a huge staff, or any staff at all, God seemingly exhausted my gifts and talents. It felt overwhelming at times, but God was using all that He put in me. Don't miss this, all of us have gifts and talents. But here is the thing, it may be that God wants to use the very seed He planted in you where you have the most doubt. God has put so many things in you of value to Him and to other people. Don't let doubt and fear to keep you from using all that is in you. Romans chapter twelve teaches us that God gives all of us gifts to use for Him, all of us!!

During the early part of writing this book, I was praying and asking the Lord what talent He wanted me to use, and then it hit me, I am using it. I am writing this book. This was the one talent I used the least. I had a few articles or poems published over the years in different places, and I kept journals and wrote lots of poems, but most of my writing I kept private. My first book, *Poetic Treasures*, I co-authored with my mother to surprise her for her birthday. The talent God was calling me to use now was the talent that I used the least. You see how God works? God has assignments for us to carry out throughout our lives. But it is important to note, we need to do it while we are able and healthy and while the circumstances allow for it to be done.

You Are Already in Position Like My Granddaddy

God needs us in a certain position, in a certain place and during a certain time so that He can manifest Himself through us. Nothing that God does is without a purpose. We discussed many Biblical characters, and I shared many stories with you, including discussing my paternal grandmother, Mamie, but allow me to share this story that I was told about my paternal grandfather, John. My grandfather's mother, like many young African American women, was raped in the early 1900's by an older white man. I am not trying to be political in any way but am merely telling the story. My great grandmother didn't have a choice and was a young girl around twelve years old. My Grandfather, John, grew up in South Carolina, and moved to Steelton, Pennsylvania, but not without grabbing his wife, my grandmother, Mamie.

By all accounts, this story was not supposed to happen the way it did, but over the years, I have interviewed relatives over and over to hear this story one more time because to me, it is quite fascinating. I need to back up a bit to tell you why my

Grandfather John went from South Carolina to Steelton. According to my family griots, my grandpa came from a family of farmers, common hard working people. But Grandpa John was somewhat of a legend in that he ended up killing white man, who tormented and killed a black man. Therefore, Grandpa John thought it prudent to get the heck out of South Carolina.

My Grandma Mamie came from a well respected, educated, and successful African American family. Yes, even during times of slavery and deep oppression, many African Americans found a way around all the racism and oppression and still manage to thrive. A lot of the racism that we see is because of a lack of knowledge and appreciation. African Americans have contributed to the intellectual wealth of the United States in math and literature; to the material and financial wealth from their free labor; and to the scientific and medical wealth from their inventions and discoveries. *"We are who we are because of who we are all."*

Back to my granddaddy's story, many in my grandma's family were teachers, and she was a teacher. She was very beautiful, and my grandfather asked for her hand in marriage. As I mentioned in a previous chapter, my grandma's parents were not too keen on my grandfather marrying into their family.

Nonetheless, she married my grandfather, had his children and, ran away with him to Steelton, Pennsylvania.

In Steelton, my grandparents ran their corner store raising ten children in the apartment on top. My grandfather turned out to be a wonderful family man fathering five boys and five girls. He was a pastor and a well-respected leader in the community. This man was a product of God's remarkable grace. He was born of a mother who was raped and redeemed from being a murderer. My grandfather's ten children were all successful in their own right in the midst of insurmountable racial disparities and other challenges. Many of his children started their own small businesses. Some went to college, and most served as deacons, pastors, evangelists and musicians in various churches throughout the United States from the east coast to the west coast.

God wants us to realize the power in our life's experiences and how He can use us in our position, in our place and during our time here on Earth so that He can manifest Himself through us. My siblings and I are the fruit of a saved and surrendered life, my Grandpa John, who refused to let his upbringing, mistakes and struggles define him. Grandpa John lived out his purpose, and God used his life to start a legacy of Christian service for the good of humanity. This is even more proof that God can use anyone, anywhere, at any time. My grandfather and my grandmother had the courageous spirit of Jael.

Sense of Urgency Like Steve Jobs

When your football team is in the fourth quarter about to make a touchdown, there is a sense of urgency because if the opposing team gets the ball, in a matter of a few good plays, in minutes the ball and game can go the other way. As believers, this is how we should live our lives. We need to understand the sense of urgency in fulfilling our purpose while we still have the strength and the will to do it. But even more importantly, our interconnectedness with the people in our lives has different timeframes.

Living through the World Pandemic COVID-19, we witnessed death all around us, which is a reminder that we don't have much time. We cannot take time for granted. Witnessing the world come to a standstill has taught us that we only really have right now, right now. Let's look at the life of the co-founder of Apple Computers, Steve Jobs (1955-2011). Jobs shocked the world with his short life when he died at the age of fifty-six.

In chronological years, he lived a short life. Yet, Steve Jobs lived with a sense of urgency and passion in carrying out what he was born to do. I am sure he did not know he would die at 56 from pancreatic cancer. However, Jobs with passion pursued all that he set out to do; even at the expense of others, who may or may not have been quite so understanding of his sense of urgency. Had he not had that sense of urgency, the two most popular inventions produced by Apple would not have been created before his death. Regardless of the struggles with his health, his legacy was sealed with two of the world's greatest inventions. In the last six years of his life, Apple launched the iPhone in 2007 and the iPad in 2010. What if Steve Jobs did not utilize his talents, gifts and skills? Our Creator has a purpose and a plan for every person, everywhere, everyday, and our lives and interconnectedness co-exists within His appointed time and place for a reason.

Nobody Can Be You But You

Earlier, we looked at the life of Jael from the Book of Judges in the Bible. As you recall, God had promised the Israelites the land, and He is not a God that breaks His Word. The military general from the opposing army, Sisera, got tired and stopped by Jael's house. He asked her for water, but she gave him milk instead, which was a very kind gesture. Jael was from a neutral tribe, but perhaps keeping up with the current events of the day, she knew of the war between the Israelites and the Canaanites. After drinking the milk, Sisera went to sleep. In that moment, Jael did what Israel's cowardly military general, Barak, could not do. Jael killed Sisera and won the war.

The battle was won and the Israelites celebrated and praised Jael as a hero. The Bible does not record any other deeds done by Jael, which is significant because she may have done a lot of wonderful things, but the lesson to know is how important our lives are to carrying out God's plan. This Biblical story helps us to understand how Jael was used to save Israel from defeat in a war and how her assignment at that appointed time saved a nation.

You were born because God needed you to carry out a specific purpose or purposes at different phases in your life. You are your son's mother, your father's daughter, your wife's husband, your patient's doctor, your student's teacher, your husband's wife, your neighbor's neighbor, your store clerk's customer, your bus driver's rider, and your friend's friend. Your life matters everyday in carrying out God's plan for each day. It is important to look at the bigger purpose and bigger picture of God's overall work in the world and know that no one can carry out your assignment but you.

Like Rosa Parks

Another example of how important it is that you carry out your assignment can be seen in the life of an African American seamstress riding home from work in Montgomery,

Alabama, at a time when African Americans were treated as second-class citizens and forced to sit in the back of the bus. Rosa Parks (1913-2005) was forty-two at the time. On December 1, 1955, tired from work and just simply wanting to go home, she got on the bus. She complied with the discriminatory laws, and she sat near the middle of the bus, just behind the ten seats reserved for white people.

But on this Thursday afternoon, it was a busy day, and all of the seats on the bus were filled. A white man came on the bus and needed a seat, and the bus driver told all four African Americans, already seated behind the white section on the bus, to move so the white man could sit down and not have to sit next to any of them. Treating African Americans in this inferior manner was a standard practice of segregation. Nonetheless, on this day, in this moment, this courageous woman quietly refused. She had been working all day, was tired. After all, she was already seated in the black section. In that moment, history was changed forever.

The bus driver called the police who came, arrested and convicted Rosa Parks for violating the laws of segregation, known as Jim Crow laws. Ms. Parks, already a local civil rights activist, appealed the conviction, which fueled a boycott of the Montgomery bus system, and challenged the inequalities in the segregated bus companies across the South. The bus boycott shook the establishment because African Americans comprised seventy-five percent of all of the bus riders. The wave of courage to stand up for what was just and fair was all embodied in this single act on December 1, 1955, when a quiet seamstress riding home from work had the courage to stand up for herself. She is now edged in the American History forever and hailed by many as the mother of the Civil Rights Movement.

Jael, Abraham, Sarah, Paul, Grandma Moses, Steve Jobs, Rosa Parks, my Grandma Mamie and my Grandpa John, all had one thing in common, God used them all. You may be thinking, wait a minute, I don't know if all of them were even Christians. I am glad you thought that because that is my point. You do not have to be a Christian to be used by God. Being redeemed by the blood of Jesus and being used by God are not synonymous. In fact, to think this is to limit God, and God can and will never be limited or reduced to human comprehension. God is able to work around the arrogance of mankind.

In Exodus, God delivered the Jews from four hundred years of captivity as slaves in Egypt. Now, God could have just orchestrated a quick and clean delivery, but he didn't. He wanted to make a statement to the Jews and to Egypt. God chose Moses to lead the Jews out of Egypt. Moses was a murderer. He was an Israelite who grew up in the palace after being adopted by the family of Pharaoh and was well loved until he killed a man who was beating a Jewish slave. Moses then fled in fear of being punished for his crime. This sounds like my Grandpa John. At any rate, God knew Moses had the experience to get the job done, and God called him out of seclusion for this task. I want to point out that just like Moses couldn't hide, we can't either. Not only is God watching us, but also in Hebrews 12:1, it lets us know that we are surrounded by witnesses. What all that means, I do not know, but I know this, God has His angels watching over us at all times, according to Psalms 91:11.

But Moses is not who I want to point out here. Pharaoh is who I want to talk about because God also used him. The Egyptians were one of the world's great superpowers in the ancient world, and the Pharaohs built great pyramids for their gods and for their loved ones to enjoy in the after life. Even today, people are baffled at how the ancient Black Egyptians built the pyramids. I have to tell you this, and then I will move on with the story. When I volunteered for a summer in Sudan, we visited the Sudanese pyramids. While visiting the Pyramids, we had an Arabic Sudanese guide. He said, "I want to point out to you that the people during that time painted these pictures, and they revealed the story of their lives at that time."

Notice," he said, "that these people were Black." I found it interesting that this Arabic man all the way in the heart of Sudan, Africa, would make such a statement of clarification.

At any rate, let's get back on track. God had been listening to the cries of His people who were in bondage. It makes sense that God would use Moses. Having grown up in the palace of the Pharaoh, we know that Moses was well known and well respected, and he had deep knowledge about the rulers, their mindset and their culture. Therefore, when Moses confronted Pharaoh, he was able to get their attention. Before God even sent Moses in to speak to Pharaoh, He told Moses in Exodus 5:21, "And the Lord said to Moses, when you go back to Egypt, see that you do all those wonders before Pharaoh which I have put in your hand. But I will harden his heart, so that he will not let the people go..."

From seeing how God dealt with Pharaoh, we learn that God can harden and soften the heart of a person at any time for His divine purpose. We can humbly and boldly go before Him in prayer understanding that He does nothing by accident. Pharaoh did not faze God. When God was good and tired of Pharaoh's arrogance and sense of control, the Lord twisted and turned Pharaoh's heart, at will for His purposes. As for Moses, God used the knowledge and experiences from his past to lead the Israelites out of Egypt. Initially, Moses doubted that he was even capable of accomplishing such a task, but God had plans for Moses' life, just like God has plans for each of our lives. Moses' assignment was to lead the Israelites out of Egypt. Because Moses was obedient in carrying out his assignment, God was glorified. God was able to manifest His awesome greatness before mankind. You can only imagine the talk of the day. Egypt has never regained prominence on the world stage.

Turn Your Mistakes Into Lessons

When you look back at all of the stories of these ordinary people, they all were just that, ordinary everyday people. Jael did not wake up and say, I am going to be forever remembered because my name will be mentioned in the Bible. Rosa Parks did not say, I am going to refuse to move today so that the world will forever look at me as the mother of the Civil Rights Movement. Then, there is Abraham. Mostly out of fear, Abraham was untruthful about Sarah being his wife to keep from being killed, and he slept with another woman because he doubted God's promise for an heir with his wife. It is certain that Abraham did not say, I am going to lie, commit adultery, throw out my first baby's momma and keep on doubting God, so I can be discussed in the Bible and show the world how I can be turned around to be used as a great man of God. Moses and my granddaddy John did not say, I am going to kill a man to protect someone else from being brutalized to be looked upon as an example of God's grace.

John 1:1-3 says this, "In the beginning was the Word, and the Word was with God, and the Word was God. The same was in the beginning with God. All things were made by Him and without Him nothing was made." In the Garden of Eden before the fall of Adam and Eve, the world was perfect. The world became imperfect because of the fall. Our imperfectness, our mistakes are a part of our human condition. The miracle of Jesus being brutalized and crucified for our sins meant that the price for all of our mistakes has been paid. In other words, Jesus knew when we were born all of the mistakes that we would make as humans, and He paved the way for our redemption. Remember, Jesus got up so that we all could get up! Our God-given assignments wherever God has placed us are not to just be carried out, but to be carried out victoriously and boldly knowing that we are on the winning side with Christ.

Hebrews 12:2 teaches us that Jesus is the author and finisher of our faith, and your mistakes can be used for His glory if you are willing to tell your story. Your life is a picture of God's redemption. Seeing the stories of others used by God, let's us know that we have the power to turn our mistakes into miracles that will help other people and even change the world in other miraculous ways. Looking at their stories also helps us to see our own impact through both our inactivity and activity. Our very presence on this planet has impact.

There are so many people doing incredible things with their lives, but none of us are immune to falling. Any of us can potentially fall flat on our face at any time. However, as we continue living out our story, there are two things that must happen. One, we need to keep rising above our mistakes. My daddy said, *"You are going to fall, but when you fall, get back up."*

We also see this same principle in Proverbs 24:16, "For a righteous man may fall seven times, and rise again, but the wicked shall fall by calamity." The other thing for us to remember is when we tell our story and show others the way to get back up, the Lord will continue to watch over and keep us as we live out our lives turning our mistakes into miracles. We can turn around our mistakes and use them as lessons to lift up other people. Remember, *"we are who we are because of who we all are."* We learn in just looking at the life of Jael and others that our connectedness makes us dependent and in need of each other and our Creator.

ENDNOTE

As someone who has devoted my life to education, I wrote this book out of an obedience to God because I believe that just like parents and the rest of society cannot expect the schools to meet all of the needs of children, the same is true about the church. Let's back up for a moment, as a person who has worked and volunteered throughout the world, I have noticed some common themes among all people, such as, we are all connected and in need of each other. In leading multicultural teams to other countries to experience and learn about different cultures, I learned the orientation started with the teams themselves really learning and understanding one other.

Back to the earlier point, we can't expect the schools alone to meet all the needs of children. These multi-billion dollar companies in all industries and organizations need to take more responsibility to work with schools to ensure that every child gets the necessary skills and employment to become financially stable adults. In the same way, Christians cannot expect the church clergy to be solely responsible for sharing the good news of the love and redemption of Jesus Christ. All of us need to do our part in every profession to share our faith and to share what the Lord has done in our lives. Jesus said in John 12:32 that if He is lifted up from the earth that He would draw all people to Himself. According to the Word, every Christian is instructed to not only study the Word of God in Second Corinthians 2:15, but also to share the gospel of Jesus Christ in Matthew 28:18-19. This would include all professions, skills and trades. We all need to come together in unity and in love because none of us can do it alone. Like Jael, God wants to use our lives to work miracles on the earth.

ACKNOWLEDGEMENTS

There are a lot of people in a lot of places that make us who we are. Sometimes these people are right up close and sometimes very far. But thank you to all my family and friends for what you mean to me. Without you in my life, how would I survive on this side of eternity? My mother and co-author of Poetic Treasures, Icie Anderson Jackson, is a source of strength and who always believed in me.

A special thanks to my father, Robert Anderson, Sr., who loved my mother, raised and guided me, and now from heaven, he is watching over me. Thanks to my sister, First Lady Brenda Anderson Fuller, who was a proofreader, and she is a best friend for me. To my friends, Patricia Hill and Christy Conklin, who proofread and supported me. To my brothers, Pastors Robert and David Anderson, who have always loved me.

But there were other friends and family, too, who lifted me up, helped me out and always encouraged me. There is a well in me that you all have helped to set free.

And my love to Cassandra Joy and Anthony Jeffries, you are the fruit of my womb and happiness for me. But the greatest thanks goes to my deepest love, the Christ of Calvary.

~Sandra Anderson, M.Ed.

ABOUT THE AUTHOR

Sandra Anderson, M.Ed., is an educator and author. She has led and trained multicultural mission's teams to different countries around the world and has served in education and in ministry for over twenty years throughout the country. Coming from a family of pastors, Anderson has a deep passion for teaching Bible studies because she believes it holds truths needed in understanding who we are and why we are here. Anderson co-authored Poetic Treasures with her mother on poems about issues across the globe. Anderson believes, like Jael, we are all a very crucial part of God's plan, and she has coined "The Jael Effect" to engulf the miracles that can occur as we embrace redemption through Christ.

References

Malcolm Gladwell, *Outliers: The Story of Success, (New York, New York, Little, Brown and Company, Hachette Book Group, 2008, pp. 48-50).*

Websites

https://en.wikipedia.org/wiki/Grandma_Moses;
https://www.wikiart.org/en/grandma-moses
https://www.biography.com/activist/rosa-parks;
https://www.biography.com/business-figure/steve-jobs